T0005155

The Outer Limits

TV Milestones Series

Series Editor

Barry Keith Grant, Brock University

TV Milestones is part of the Contemporary
Approaches to Film and Media Series

———————————————

A complete listing of the books in this series can
be found online at wsupress.wayne.edu.

The Outer Limits

Joanne Morreale

Wayne State University Press
Detroit

ISBN (paperback): 978-0-8143-4745-4
ISBN (ebook): 978-0-8143-4746-1

Library of Congress Control Number: 2021943179

Cover art © ANDREY-SHA74 / Shutterstock.com.

Wayne State University Press rests on Waawiyaataanong, also referred to as Detroit, the ancestral and contemporary homeland of the Three Fires Confederacy. These sovereign lands were granted by the Ojibwe, Odawa, Potawatomi, and Wyandot nations, in 1807, through the Treaty of Detroit. Wayne State University Press affirms Indigenous sovereignty and honors all tribes with a connection to Detroit. With our Native neighbors, the press works to advance educational equity and promote a better future for the earth and all people.

Wayne State University Press
Leonard N. Simons Building
4809 Woodward Avenue
Detroit, Michigan 48201-1309

Visit us online at wsupress.wayne.edu.

CONTENTS

ACKNOWLEDGMENTS

I n the late 1960s I'd watch *The Outer Limits* on Saturday afternoons with my brother Frank. It came on right after *Candlepins for Cash* and right before *Creature Feature*, which seemed to make some kind of crazy sense. After the somnambulant rhythms of strikes and spares filmed in close-up slow motion, I liked being jolted by *The Outer Limits'* scary opening, monsters, and special effects. It wasn't until much later that I realized that the series was also about ideas. When I found myself teaching Television History a few years ago, I came back to *The Outer Limits*—and I especially want to thank two students, Julie Ryu and Mariel Segovia, for sharing my enthusiasm for early television and inspiring me to keep exploring it. Penny Sander, Rufus Seder, Paul Rocklin, Bonnie Waltch and Richard Lewis watched episodes with me, kindly shared their insights, and patiently listened to mine. My thanks also to David Schow who generously shared his time and expertise on *The Outer Limits*.

Annie Martin and Barry Grant gave me initial encouragement to pursue a project on *The Outer Limits*, and it has been a pleasure to work with editor Marie Sweetman. Thanks too to Carrie Downes Teefey, Emily Shelton, and Lucas Freeman for their help in seeing the manuscript through to completion. A special nod to Rufus Seder for his technical help—he is a magician! I also appreciate the thoughtful suggestions made by Barry Grant and two anonymous reviewers that helped make this a better book.

I am sorry to say goodbye to *The Outer Limits'* universe. I can't help but feel there is still much to learn.

INTRODUCTION

The television screen becomes an oscillating sine wave, accompanied by a discordant noise. The picture flickers, suggesting that the set is on the blink. The portentous tone of an off-screen Control Voice assures us this is not the case:

> There is nothing wrong with your television set. Do not attempt to adjust the picture. We are controlling transmission. We will control the horizontal. We will control the vertical. We can change the focus to a soft blur or sharpen it to crystal clarity. For the next hour, sit quietly and we will control all that you see and hear. You are about to participate in a great adventure. You are about to witness the awe and mystery which reaches from the inner mind . . . to the outer limits.

As the voice proclaims that an unidentified "we" have the ability to manipulate electronic signals, the images on screen mimic signal interference patterns. This self-reflexive opening to *The Outer Limits* (ABC, 1963–65) marks it as different from typical television programs on the air in the 1960s. By calling attention to the medium, it disrupts flow and inverts assumptions about the relationship between viewers and television. Instead of reinforcing perceptions of television as a familiar, benevolent technology that provides a

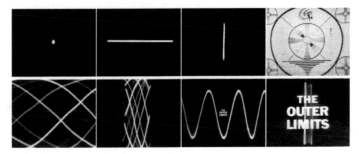

Images from *The Outer Limits* opening credits.

window onto the world, the opening reminds viewers that television is in fact an "alien" object that controls what they see.

At a time when television was still new, the implication that unknown forces lurking behind the screen could control transmission was disturbing, to say the least. At the same time, the Control Voice tantalizes viewers by promising that those who participate in the "great adventure" will witness awe and mystery. The segment jolts viewers at the same time that it entices them; in this way, it serves as a metaphor for the series itself, where form and content work to simultaneously unsettle and enthrall.

The Outer Limits was a science fiction/horror anthology series that explored the relationship between humans and technology. In contrast to the array of game shows, crime series, sitcoms, and westerns on television in 1963, *The Outer Limits* presented fantastical worlds in order to comment upon the real world. Episodes addressed anxieties born of Cold War politics in the post–World War II era, especially as they manifested in concerns about technology and the perennial science fiction question of what it means to be human. As illustrated by the opening credits, television itself represented the threatening nature of technology. Horrock sums up its meaning in this period:

> Since the 1950s the television set represented technological competition, electronic surveillance, consumer psychology, the rise of corporate culture, and post-war philosophies of alienation and existence. The anxieties of the arms and space race, and the literature that imagined the future cast as a surveillance state in which technology would dominate, turned the television into an object of suspicion, and a suspicious object. (103)

By "taking control" of the television set, *The Outer Limits* aroused fears of the power of the medium that were exacerbated by individual episodes. Producer Joseph Stefano's fifteen-page guide for writers, "The Canons of *Please Stand By*" (*Please Stand By* was the original title of the show), described it as "a one-hour, dramatic television series whose dramas are woven upon the inventive and imaginative loom of Science Fiction"; most important, he added that some of the loom's "threads" were themes such as conformity, discrimination, politics, censorship, disarmament, man's inaccessibility to man, moral-physical slavery, mass culture, and peace (Schow, 1998, 353). Its themes illustrated how science fiction could serve as a source of socioeconomic, political, and cultural critique, while its aesthetic strategies demonstrated the way form and content worked together. As Booker observes, "At its best, it was as literate, thought-provoking, and multi-layered as anything ever to appear on network tv" (2004, 21).

Despite attracting a core of devoted viewers during its initial run, *The Outer Limits* became more popular after it went off the air. Over the years, it developed a cult following, due to its near-constant syndication in the United States as well as the UK, Canada, and Australia. There have been several DVD releases, most recently a digitally remastered Blu-ray edition in 2018, and, as of this writing, the series is available on popular streaming sites such as iTunes, Amazon, and

Hulu. A reboot aired on Showtime from 1995 to 2001, with a final season on the SYFY network from 2001 to 2002. As I argue in chapter 5, the later version was primarily an exercise in branding, designed to attract fans of the original along with new viewers, and as such it was essentially a different program that did not reproduce the artistic vision of its source text. But still today the original *Outer Limits* maintains a social media presence on platforms such as Twitter, YouTube, Facebook, and Reddit, as well as on blogs and fan websites. As with all television programs with an avid fan base, through the years brand extensions have expanded upon or remediated *The Outer Limits'* story world—critical guides and companions, novelizations of episodes, a children's book series, comic books, trading cards, T-shirts, a board game, a music soundtrack, and collector's-item replicas of monsters.

Despite its longevity and importance to television history, *The Outer Limits* has received little scholarly attention. David Schow's *The Outer Limits Companion* (1998) provides extensive information on the production background and various episodes; this book owes a great debt to it, but Schow does not endeavor to locate *The Outer Limits* as a television milestone. More recently, Reba A. Wissner's *We Will Control All That Your Hear* (2016) provides an extraordinary account of sound and music in the series, though her work primarily focuses on that aspect. Indeed, there have been scant studies of science fiction television, with the bulk of the work devoted to *The Twilight Zone* (CBS, 1959–64), the show to which *The Outer Limits* is often compared (episodes of the two series are often confused).

While *The Twilight Zone* and *The Outer Limits* share thematic similarities, *The Outer Limits* is more firmly rooted in science fiction, though it simultaneously engages with a variety of styles and genres, particularly Gothic horror. *The Outer Limits* typically heightens anxieties; in contrast, as Grant observes, *Twilight Zone* episodes are often morality tales that ultimately resolve the anxieties they raise (86). *The Twilight Zone* frequently relies on twist endings to foster critical thought, while episodes of *The Outer Limits* aim to shock and frighten viewers, whether through the opening credits, startling and inventive special effects, monsters and aliens, eerie sonics, or narratives that end on an unresolved or pessimistic note. *The Outer Limits* is also more formally experimental than *The Twilight Zone*. As Stefano asserts in "The Canons," "A high literary style encompassing the bold use of poetic imagery and stunning language is entirely fitting and not unnatural to the Science Fiction form" (Schow 1998, 353). Its aesthetics draw from theater and cinema, particularly expressionism, the Gothic, and surrealism, all of which are employed to convey an atmosphere of pervasive dread, attempting to disrupt and unsettle rather than reassure viewers. In *The Outer Limits*, unbridled science and faith in technology create horror; science and technology exceed our ability to control them, and human fear of the unknown and propensity to destroy what it does not understand has dire consequences.

Production Background

The Outer Limits was an anomaly in the context of television in the early 1960s. It combined science fiction and horror at a time when family-friendly programs dominated the airwaves; it was an anthology at a time when television had largely transitioned to series with recurring characters and formulaic plots; and its bleak narratives contrasted with the upbeat episodes that typified the majority of programs on the air. As I elaborate upon in chapter 1, producers Leslie Stevens and Joseph Stefano took advantage of popular perceptions that science fiction and horror were not "serious," which enabled them—for a time—to keep under the radar of network executives and sponsors.

The Outer Limits came on the air because ABC, the lowest-rated network in the late 1950s and 1960s, decided to appeal to audience segments rather than compete with CBS and NBC (Baughman 2007, 281). *The Outer Limits* would build on the success of two outliers that appealed to distinct audiences: *The Twilight Zone*, then approaching its final season, and *Alfred Hitchcock Presents* (1962–65), a suspense-based anthology in its second season. A television program oriented toward science fiction more than fantasy or suspense resonated with the Kennedy administration's focus on science, technology, and space exploration.

The Outer Limits was created by Leslie Stevens (1924–98), who was originally a playwright and acolyte of Orson Welles. Like many playwrights at a time when the television industry was based in New York, he simultaneously wrote for televised dramatic anthologies. From 1955 to 1959 he wrote for *Playhouse 90* (CBS 1956–60), a prestigious television anthology series known for socially relevant and often controversial material. But, as I discuss in chapter 1, by the mid-1950s the center of the television industry was shifting from New York to Hollywood, and live dramatic anthologies became supplanted by telefilms that were cheaper to produce and more suited to a commercial medium. Like many television writers, Stevens moved to Hollywood and in 1959 founded his own independent film production company, Daystar (initially along with talent agent Stanley Colbert). He wrote, produced, and directed three films, the most notable being *Private Property* (1960) which critics associated with both film noir and the French New Wave art film. I briefly discuss *Private Property* in chapter 4 as an example of the way Stevens's artistic aspirations informed his approach to *The Outer Limits*.

Stevens returned to television in 1961, stating that he wanted to provide continuous employment for what he termed his "Blue Ribbon" production crew (Schow 1998, 15). Like other independent television companies, Daystar partnered with a Hollywood production company, in this case United Artists. They first produced *Stoney Burke* (ABC 1962–63), an unconventional television western about rodeo riders that was canceled after one season. When Stevens was unable to sell other television pilots, United Artists' vice president of programming, Richard Dorso, suggested that he try a science fiction program.

In some ways, a science fiction anthology program was an odd choice. There were few anthology series still on the air by 1963. Moreover, televised science fiction was typically aimed at one of two audience segments: children, as with shows such as *Captain Video and His Space Rangers* (DuMont 1949–55), or fans of science-based stories, as was the case with *Science Fiction Theater* (syndicated, 1955–57). At first, *The Outer Limits* attempted to align itself with *Science Fiction Theater*, as was apparent in a publicity release: "Each episode of *The Outer Limits* begins with a scientific fact. That fact is dramatized, illumined, projected into the Future and developed into a highly imaginative yet believable adventure . . . the swift developments in space, electronics, 'miracle medicine' and atomics provide fresh stimuli for the creative dramatist, and bring 'the unknown' more frighteningly close, more fascinatingly real" (Schow 1998, 2).

Connecting the show to *Science Fiction Theater* placed it within a familiar generic tradition, and likely reassured ABC that the show would be conventional, though the ensuing blend of science fiction and horror did not conform to this format. More likely, Stevens, who described himself as a "creative dramatist," related to a third type of science fiction: stories adapted by well-known authors such as Ray Bradbury or Judith Merril that had appeared on anthology programs such as *Playhouse 90* (Yascek 2008, 57). These latter stories exemplified science fiction as an intellectual and artistic endeavor; as Canavan and Link write, "Since WWI science fiction has been the genre of choice for authors who wanted the narrative freedom to explore new ideas and new philosophies in compelling, challenging, and provocative ways, as well as to talk back against the trends of contemporary culture" (2015, 10). But Stevens was well aware of the creative constraints imposed by a commercial medium. As he stated, "I wanted to stress, dwell on, and get into the dimensions, other beings, and alien

7

stuff that truly went to the outer limits of the imagination. Now, you can only do that for so long until you begin to hear, 'uh—you're getting pretty far out, there. That may be interesting to a handful of people, but can you bring it down to earth so that the big numbers, the masses, will understand?" (Schow 1998, 24). The disparity between Stevens's vision of the program and what ABC wanted would intensify throughout the first season, especially after Joseph Stefano (1922–2006) joined Stevens as coproducer and became what today would be called the showrunner.

After hearing Stevens's pitch, ABC asked him to make a pilot. He made it at a cost of $213,000, a reasonable budget at the time. But to encourage ABC to pick up the series, Stevens contacted Stefano to become coproducer, offering him both creative and decision-making control. Stevens was likely aware that a coproducer would improve his chances of selling the series; the networks were wary of independent companies headed by a "hyphenate"—a single producer and writer—who might rebel against their dictates. It was also the case that ABC might be reluctant to greenlight a series from a producer whose earlier work (*Stoney Burke*) had been canceled.

In a fortuitous coincidence, ABC had been courting Stefano to work on a television project at the same time that Stevens reached out to him (Schow 1998, 40). Like Stevens, Stefano had been a writer for dramatic anthologies, in this case *General Electric Theater* (1953–62) as well as *Playhouse 90*. But Stefano was best known as the screenwriter for Alfred Hitchcock's *Psycho* (1960), which established the genre of the psychological horror film and exerted a strong influence on Stefano's work on *The Outer Limits*. While most accounts of this period of television history emphasize the rivalries between film and television, in chapter 1 I elaborate on the way Stevens and Stefano moved between industries and brought their cinematic sensibilities, as well as their commitment to science fiction as social commentary, to *The Outer Limits*.

Stefano incorporated as Villa di Stefano Productions in order to become a full partner with Daystar and United Artists. Once Stefano signed on, he became the show's hands-on producer. Stevens wrote, directed, and produced four episodes while Stefano wrote fourteen episodes in the first season, rewrote scenes in almost every episode except for those written by Stevens, and was responsible for writing virtually all of the opening and closing Control Voice narrations (Schow 1998, 80). Many of his episodes were made with cinematographer Conrad Hall and director Gerd Oswald, both of whom had backgrounds in film and brought expressionist film techniques to television. In chapter 2 I discuss *The Outer Limits*' visual style, which stood apart from other network television fare in 1963–64. As Schow summarizes, "Their series would blend science fiction and Gothic horror in literate screenplays well filmed *as* film, eschewing the prosaic techniques of TV and running contrary to the medium's entropic flow of dullness" (1998, 3).

Stefano wrote "The Canons of *Please Stand By*" after ABC requested a theme statement for the show. (*Please Stand By* was the original title.) "The Canons" satisfied ABC's desire to avoid material that was too cerebral. For example, one executive told Stevens to "aim for the throat, heart, belly, groin—but never the head" (Schow 1998, 24). Stefano also agreed to ABC's request for monsters in every episode so that the show would appeal to both youthful viewers as well as science fiction fans. Stefano's "Canons" referred to monsters as the BEAR: "Each play must have a 'BEAR.' The BEAR is that one splendid, staggering, shuddering effect that induces awe or wonder or tolerable terror or even merely conversation and argument" (Schow 1998, 354). Occasionally, though, the twist was that the BEAR would be the human rather than the creature on the screen.

ABC also objected to the show's title, *Please Stand By*. At the height of Cold War tensions and less than a year after the Cuban Missile Crisis, they feared that it was too similar to the Emergency Broadcast

Alert (Schow 1998, 53). Stevens settled on *The Outer Limits*, a title that evoked *The Twilight Zone*, with "the outer limits of the imagination" replacing Serling's notion of a fifth dimension that was as "vast as space and as timeless as infinity." Stevens also asked Stefano to serve as on-screen host to introduce the show. The host, a convention of anthology series, provided name recognition, identified themes, and served as a point of identification for viewers, whether it be Truman Bradley on *Science Fiction Theater*, Boris Karloff on *Thriller* (1960–62), Roald Dahl on *Way Out* (1961), Alfred Hitchcock on *Alfred Hitchcock Presents*, or Rod Serling—who appeared on-screen from season 2 onward—on *The Twilight Zone*. When Stefano declined, Stevens developed the idea for what became known as the Control Voice to open and close each episode. Rather than providing the familiarity and reassurance of typical on-camera hosts, narrator Vic Perrin's voice began by "taking control" of the television set. The opening credit sequence was disturbing, unlike anything else seen on television, and just right for *The Outer Limits*.

Throughout the series' run, the writers, directors, cinematographers, musical composers, actors, and even sound and special effects teams were some of the best in television. Conrad Hall, named one of Hollywood's ten most influential cinematographers by the International Cinematographers Guild in 2003, began his career on *The Outer Limits*. According to Hall, "Anything I ever heard about, dreamt about, or thought up—I tried everything in the book. *The Outer Limits* became a school for the development of my craft" (Schow 1998, 21). His camera operator was William Fraker, who went on to become cinematographer on the films *Bullitt* (1968) and *Rosemary's Baby* (1968). The two most frequent directors were Gerd Oswald (fourteen episodes) and Byron Haskin (six episodes). Oswald directed the noir classic *A Kiss Before Dying* (1956), while Haskin's most famous film was *The War of the Worlds* (1953). In addition to Stevens and Stefano, well-known writers such as Meyer Dolinsky, Charles Beaumont, Robert Towne, Anthony Lawrence, Jerry Sohl, and, in season 2, Harlan Ellison and Robert

Dennis, worked on the show. Jancovich refers to several of these as part of a group of writers who were working to transform horror and fantasy, "often through an emphasis on psychologized dramas played out in relatively realistic settings" (2018, 22). He names *Psycho* as the film that changed everything, with the television anthology programs that followed an important part of the shift to psychological horror. He cites *Thriller*, *Alfred Hitchcock Presents*, and *The Twilight Zone* as three examples, though he inexplicably neglects *The Outer Limits*, whose producer was the writer for *Psycho*.

Dominic Frontiere, Robert Van Eps, John Elizalde, and, in season 2, Harry Lubin composed original music and created sound effects. *The Outer Limits* was the first television program to hire a special effects company, Project Unlimited, to create monsters and props. *The Outer Limits* also featured well-known actors such as Cliff Robertson, Robert Culp, Diana Sands, David McCallum, Gloria Grahame, Bruce Dern, Vera Miles, Martin Sheen, Neil Hamilton, James Shigeta, Eddie Albert, Robert Duvall, Martin Landau, Sally Kellerman, Chita Rivera, Carroll O'Connor, and Ed Asner. Leonard Nimoy and William Shatner, who went on to *Star Trek* (CBS, 1966–69) fame, also appeared on the show.

Despite *The Outer Limits*' high-quality writing, acting, cinematography, and direction, its macabre visuals and pessimistic tone were not to ABC's liking. Midway through the first season, the network asked Stevens and Stefano to "tailor the show to more conventional tastes" so that it would have more mainstream appeal, though neither complied (Holcomb 2002) Although the show was popular with teenagers and young adults, it failed to break into the top 30 in the Nielsen ratings. According to Stevens, it was a "bleeder": a show that wasn't quite in the hit column but wasn't exactly a failure, either (Schow 1998, 235). Though it finished with a 19.0 rating at a time when a rating of 16.0 was the baseline for renewal, ABC at first considered canceling it and then decided to move it from Monday nights at 7:30 p.m. to Saturday nights at 7:30 for its second season. They scheduled it opposite

The Jackie Gleason Show (CBS, 1962–65), then the most popular show on television, and *Flipper* (NBC, 1964–67), which would compete with younger viewers. Stefano, aware that the scheduling change—and concurrent budget cuts—would doom the show, left at the end of season 1; Stevens followed soon after. They were replaced by Ben Brady, an ABC executive who turned the second season into more conventional science fiction.

Season 2 of *The Outer Limits* exemplifies how the autonomy of the independent writer-producer became circumscribed as the networks expanded their control of production and program ownership. On the one hand, the industry depended on independent production companies such as Daystar for innovative ideas. As Alvey writes, "Whether driven by creativity or desperation, independents, both in feature films and telefilms—were willing to take chances that the convention-minded and tradition bound studios were not" (1997, 151). Under the stewardship of Stevens and Stefano, *The Outer Limits* expanded both the aesthetic and narrative conventions of television. At the same time, their relationship with ABC was precarious. The networks were resistant to producers having too much control (as I discuss in chapter 1), especially when, as in the case of *The Outer Limits*, their programs were considered too unconventional, too expensive, and too low in ratings.

As a result, when Stefano quit, United Artists recommended that ABC hire their vice president of programming, Ben Brady, to replace him, largely because they knew that, as a former executive, he would keep the show on budget (Schow 1998, 240). Brady, initially a producer who made the transition to management, was best known for his collaboration with author Erle Stanley Gardner to create *Perry Mason* (ABC, 1957–66), after which he produced the first sixty-eight episodes. As ABC's vice president of programming, he held a supervisory role on *The Outer Limits*, but Brady's work was representative of the Hollywood model based on maximizing profit rather than expressing an artistic vision. As producer of season 2, he was more accommodating to network demands than Stevens or Stefano. Director Gerd Oswald, one of the few creative personnel to stay on after Stevens and Stefano left the show at the end of season 1, compared the two: "Whereas Stefano would say of an idea, 'Great, let's do it and I'll fight the network later,' Brady would say, 'I'd like to, but I can't'" (Schow 1998, 241).

As Brady surmised with regard to the first season of *The Outer Limits*, "A good deal of the first year was a banner year in terms of art and product. Stefano was a great writer. But there was a violent schism between what he wanted and what the network wanted" (Schow 2018, 2). In contrast, Brady defined his approach: "We sought out published works by established science fiction writers. We looked for a marriage between intelligent science fiction and good, sound showmanship" (2). But ABC cut the show's budget to $100,000 per episode, which limited the amount they could pay for a story. In addition, ABC demanded that episodes still have monsters, though the reduced budget meant that the visual and optical effects that distinguished the first season were extremely limited. Neither Dominic Frontiere or Conrad Hall, who had contributed to the rich sound and visuals of the first season, worked on the second season. Jack Poplin, a crew member who worked on both seasons, summarized the disparity between the two: "The first season was far more creative and esoteric than the second, which was much more commercial. Ben Brady is a capable man, but an executive, not a creator. He was doing what he was told and grinding them out. He was out of his depth, with the onus of the heavyweights who had preceded him" (Schow 1998, 247).

As a result of the change in producers, season 2 was different than season 1. While television is always a collaborative process, the producer is the creative force who shapes material into a coherent form. Without Stefano at the helm, season 2 lacked the artistic vision that made season 1 so remarkable. This monograph thus pays closer attention to season 1, in order to portray *The Outer Limits* as television milestone. While season 1 consisted of thirty-two episodes, season 2 lasted only seventeen episodes and was canceled mid-season due to low ratings, leaving behind several episodes that have never been aired.

The Outer Limits as Television Milestone

The Outer Limits has much to offer both television fans and scholars. It engages those who want to understand how television writers adapted as the locus of the industry shifted from New York to Hollywood, and it illuminates a previously little-known aspect of the relation of dramatic anthologies to horror and science fiction. It shows how science fiction and horror work as social commentary, illustrates the connection between film, theater, and television aesthetics, and demonstrates how television programs adapt and build on previous works while providing insight into the way television texts link to the past, interact with one another and relate to future programs. In chapter 1, I explore the relationship between live dramatic anthologies—which were the "prestige programming" of early television—and less well-regarded genre fiction. The first season of *The Outer Limits* bears a direct lineage to dramatic anthologies through Stevens and Stefano. While writers for dramatic anthologies were often committed to making socially relevant art, they were discouraged from doing so as the television industry became more conservative and commercially driven. Genre fiction allowed Stevens and Stefano to express a creative vision and make social commentary at time when the industry wanted programming that would not disturb or offend viewers.

Chapter 2 considers the series as a specifically *televisual* program at a time when most programs eschewed excessive style. *The Outer Limits* expanded the possibilities of the medium by merging spectacular images characteristic of science fiction with the theatricality of live television and expressionist techniques drawn from cinema, especially those associated with film noir, Gothic horror, and surrealism.

In this chapter I focus on two episodes, "Nightmare," and "The Bellero Shield," as examples of how *The Outer Limits* expanded the aesthetic possibilities of television in a manner that disrupted a seamless viewing experience. While "Nightmare" heightens anxieties through "noir science fiction," "The Bellero Shield" is "Gothic science fiction" that relies on the atmospherics of horror. Before most television programs paid attention to the relation of form and content, *The Outer Limits* demonstrated the interplay of word, sound, and image to provoke and disturb viewers.

In chapter 3, I consider *The Outer Limits'* use of science fiction to convey its vision of a society coping with social and technological change in the midst of the Cold War and the Kennedy administration's "New Frontier." Here I discuss the series pilot, "The Galaxy Being," which addresses fear of space exploration and the power of television in a story that displays scientific endeavor gone awry. The episode provides a self-reflexive commentary on the medium of television and introduces the dire warnings that recur throughout season 1: technology is out of control, humans are more monstrous than the monsters, and humans' fear and aggression will lead to their downfall. "OBIT," while on the one hand a critique of Cold War politics, develops *The Outer Limits'* critique of television and addresses issues such as loss of privacy, electronic surveillance, the rise of the military-industrial complex, and the seductive power of media. Finally, "Architects of Fear" takes on the theme of identity that runs throughout much science fiction; it contemplates the boundaries between human and nonhuman as it simultaneously provokes concerns about nuclear holocaust, extraterrestrial invasion, and the misguided use of science.

Chapter 4 addresses *The Outer Limits'* use of creative adaptation. Like many science fiction television series where writers were under pressure to produce new material under tight deadlines and constrained budgets, *The Outer Limits* often drew from previously published stories, films, or even other television shows. It illustrates the propensity for science fiction to recycle familiar material as well as the difficulty of establishing ownership of an idea. I expand upon this point by describing the dispute between *Outer Limits* writer Harlan Ellison and James Cameron, who directed the film *The Terminator* (1984), as well as charges that writer Alan Moore used ideas from *The Outer Limits* in his comics series *Watchmen* (1986–87). But I also argue that *The Outer Limits*, itself a hybrid of the "low culture" genres of science fiction and horror, disrupted narrative and aesthetic conventions by borrowing from "high" culture forms such as classic literature, surrealism, and art cinema. Here I discuss "The Guests," one of *The Outer Limits*' most unusual episodes, which draws upon multiple sources (television, literature, Gothic melodrama, and surrealism), and "The Forms of Things Unknown," a loose adaptation of the French art film *Les Diaboliques* (1955) that also evokes Shakespeare's *A Midsummer Night's Dream*. The latter episode—the final one aired in Season 1—was Stefano's attempt to bring the art film to television, a move that demonstrated the limits of experimentation on network television and led to the end of Stevens and Stefano's reign on *The Outer Limits*.

The monograph concludes by considering *The Outer Limits*' influence upon later endeavors. One of its most important connections was to the original *Star Trek*, with which it shared some of the same writers, directors, actors, props, and even stories. While *Star Trek* similarly used science fiction as a vehicle for social commentary, its progressive representations and visions of a utopian future reversed the pessimism of *Outer Limits* narratives. I then suggest that *The X-Files'* (1993–2002) expression of an authorial vision, mix of science fiction and horror, and visual aesthetics, which legitimated it as "quality" television in the 1990s, can be traced back to *The Outer Limits*. *The X-Files'* success facilitated the making of the new *Outer Limits*, but I suggest that the new series limited rather than expanded artistic innovation and notions of quality. By comparing two versions of *The Outer Limits'* "A Feasibility Study," which Stefano wrote in 1964 and then updated for the new show in 1997, I illustrate how the latter episode served to accommodate rather than critique its social and political milieu. I conclude with a discussion of the dystopian science fiction series *Black Mirror* (2012) as a contemporary version of *The Outer Limits*. Like its predecessor, *Black Mirror* critiques our reliance on technology and the way it manifests in modern society. The relation between *The Outer Limits* and *Black Mirror* shows how fundamental questions about human nature, and whether we control our technologies or whether they control us, continue to percolate through the culture.

1

HIGHBROW MEETS LOWBROW

In this chapter, I explore the relation between *The Outer Limits* and the form of the dramatic television anthology as a key to understanding Stevens and Stefano's commitment to science fiction as a vehicle for social and political commentary, as well as to illuminate the connections of their work to theater and film. Science fiction allowed Stevens and Stefano to express their vision and promote thought at a time when the industry wanted bland programming that would not challenge viewers. In the guise of genre fiction, *The Outer Limits* addressed the anxieties of the age: ambivalence about technology, Cold War politics, and the human condition. By turning to "lowbrow" science fiction and horror, Stevens and Stefano provided critical cultural commentary while operating within the commercial constraints of television; conversely, their work on *The Outer Limits* showed how marginalized genres such as science fiction and horror both entertained viewers and provoked them to ponder larger questions.

From the Live Dramatic Anthology to the Telefilm

At first glance, live dramatic anthologies and science fiction programs would seem to have little in common. Dramatic anthology series, which dominated television from 1947 to 1955, first appeared as 19 the nascent television industry experimented with different kinds of programs. The radio networks (CBS, NBC, ABC, and DuMont) that came to preside over television emulated familiar programming formats, which included anthology series aimed at adults. Moreover, "serious" programs that were essentially filmed plays enabled the networks to present television as a vehicle for high culture while also establishing live programming as its ideal aesthetic, and so to differentiate it from film (Vianello 2013, 11). According to Baughman, "There was every expectation that in some form the anthology drama would become a permanent part of the television schedule. The anthology drama had been a network radio staple. Large corporations like U.S. Steel, Alcoa, and Armstrong were willing to be sole sponsors. Such programs were thought to possess a prestige other types of TV fare—the comic variety show or situation comedy—lacked" (2007, 177). The dramatic anthology series helped establish television's aesthetic of liveness and immediacy, as well as to position it as a vehicle for transmitting culture. At a time when the industry was based in New York, it was natural to turn to the theater for material, especially given the similarities between theatrical and television productions. Television programs were broadcast live, and so, like plays, they were confined to a few settings on a single stage. As a result, many were structured through the Aristotelian unities of time, place, and action: they took place in real time, in one or two locations, and had one main action, all of which helped to convey a sense of realism to viewers watching in their homes (Kraszewski 2010, 73). In lieu of action, television dramas focused on character, conflict, and emotion, which were easily conveyed by the close-up.

Multiple factors contributed to making dramatic anthologies such as *The Kraft Television Theater* (1947–57), *Westinghouse Studio One* (1948–58), *The Philco-Goodyear Television Playhouse* (1948–56), *General Electric Theater*, and *Playhouse 90* "prestige" programs: the status accorded to theater; the well-known playwrights and actors who moved from theater to television to write, produce, and act in anthology programs; and challenging, often controversial, subject matter. Kraszewski writes that at a time when theater attendance was in decline, "many theater people thought that the technological capabilities of television could advance a national project of enlightenment by transmitting the arts of New York City across the nation" (2010, 30). Even many television executives, most notably NBC president Pat Weaver, initially envisioned television as a harbinger of sophisticated tastes in postwar culture rather than a mass-entertainment medium. Both the networks and the sponsors of their programs promoted the high-culture value of dramatic anthologies; as Everett states, they "turned to dramatic shows as a programming strategy to elevate the status of television and attract the growing and increasingly important suburban audience" (2013, 1001).

Initially, producers of critically acclaimed anthologies hired writers to adapt Broadway plays, classic dramas, or short stories, although gradually they realized that it was easier and cheaper for writers to develop their own material. As there were no requirements regarding character, location, or formula, writers had a great deal of creative autonomy. According to Barnouw, "Writers responded to the open invitation of these series in a way that gave television for some years the initiative among dramatic media and made it the mecca of young writers and the source of other media" (1962, 35). In theater, authorship was ascribed to writers rather than producers or directors, and this practice continued with the writers of dramatic anthologies, who were called television playwrights. Kraszewski describes many of these writers as new entrepreneurs. In the conservative milieu of the late 1950s and early 1960s, he writes, they "often behaved like new entrepreneurs in order to inject liberal politics into their scripts, liberal politics they could not otherwise advocate in the 1950s television industry" (12). He adds that television anthology writers often circulated between theater, film, print, and television and so were not beholden to one program, studio, or medium. If a script was rejected, a writer could always reimagine it for a different medium.

Many of the most well-known television anthology writers—including Gore Vidal, Reginald Rose, Horton Foote, and Paddy Chayefsky—were committed to writing the same kind of socially relevant material for television that they did for theater, as was Rod Serling, who built his career writing for television rather than the stage. According to Newcomb, "The focus on psychological realism of so-called 'ordinary' characters, on contemporary settings, on non-formulaic narrative structures, and for most early television critics, on probing particular types of social problems elevated some of the early live dramas on television into exemplary texts" (1997, 108). Notably, in 1959 Stefano won a Robert E. Sherwood Award, given to television programs dedicated to advancing social freedom and justice, for his script for "Made in Japan," a *Playhouse 90* drama about racial prejudice. In a 1964 interview, Stefano suggested that he and Stevens continued to develop this approach in *The Outer Limits*, commenting, "If there is one message in the show, it's a strong preachment against violence, bigotry, and prejudice" (quoted in Wissner 2016, 7).

Live dramatic anthologies such as *Kraft Television Theatre*, *Philco-Goodyear Television Playhouse*, or *Westinghouse Studio One* only remained television staples as long as the industry was based in New York. But by the 1956–57 season, Hollywood had overtaken New York as the center of the television industry, and by 1960, over 80 percent of the prime-time schedule was generated in Hollywood (Alvey 1997, 139). The transition occurred gradually throughout the 1950s. At first, the networks believed that filmed programs were too expensive because viewers would not want to watch them more than once. Despite these reservations, the major film studios began to develop telefilms in the 1940s, though they were slow to embrace the new medium. Partly they were wrangling (in vain) with the FCC for a more lucrative model of subscription television that involved showing programs in theaters. Also, despite the government's 1948 antitrust decree that forced the five major studios—Paramount, Metro-Goldwyn Mayer, Warner Bros., Twentieth Century Fox, and RKO Radio Pictures—to separate production and distribution from exhibition, full separation did not occur until 1959, so the film studios did not want to alienate theater owners who might resent their participation in television and refuse to show their films.

Despite the film industry's desire to remain separate from television, the breakup of the studio system left them with unused sound stages and back lots. Since telefilms gave the studios a financial boost, in the mid-1950s both Columbia Pictures and Universal set up television production arms. In addition, the United Paramount theater chain, no longer able to invest in film, bought the third-place ABC network in 1953 and differentiated it from CBS and NBC by making filmed television programs—most successfully, *Disneyland* (1954–58), later renamed *Walt Disney Presents* (1958–61). As a result, Anderson writes, "by the end of the 1950s, with the fates of the networks and studios deeply entwined, filmed television series emerged as the dominant product of the Hollywood studios and the dominant form of prime-time programming" (1994, 7).

Concurrent with the film industry's slow crawl to television in the 1950s, the television networks came to realize that telefilms were more profitable than live television. Although they played lip service to live television as aesthetically and culturally superior to telefilms, they learned that they could make money from reruns, syndication, and foreign sales. In addition, sponsors were becoming more averse to the controversial, often downbeat content in many of the dramatic anthology programs. As the 1950s wore on, fewer dramatic anthology series were made; as Sander writes, "a small window of creative opportunity began to close, and TV playwrights were faced with increasing censorship from timorous ad agencies and broadcasting executives" (quoted in Telotte 2008, 113). Sponsors pressured anthology writers to produce "acceptable" works that avoided complicated depictions of human frailty or that had unhappy or ambiguous endings. According to Barnouw, they became "increasingly intent on interfering with script matters, dictating changes, vetoing plot details"

(1975, 165). Filmed episodic programs with recurring characters, formulaic plots, and happy endings were more compatible with television's commercial imperatives. Characters that served as points of identification were more likely to draw repeat viewers, and upbeat endings that offered clear resolutions to problems reinforced advertising messages. In a context where the networks adopted a "least offensive programming" model in order to placate sponsors and attract mainstream viewers, most television tended to be bland, formulaic, and escapist. Frederick Ziv, creator of *The Cisco Kid*, explained, "It was obvious to all of us who had our finger on the pulse of the American public that they wanted escapist entertainment. . . . We did not do highbrow material. We did material that would appeal to the broadest segment of the public" (Boddy 1993, 72).

The Television Writer: From Highbrow to Lowbrow

As television shifted from live to filmed programming, the television playwright lost ground to network executives and sponsors, whose main objective was to reach as many viewers as possible. Barnouw lamented the change in 1957: "Diversity was vanishing; series after series was a carbon copy. Crime formula dominated almost all schedules . . . It was especially catastrophic for the future of the medium that the 'anthology series' seemed in danger of disappearing" (1962, 35). By 1959, *Playhouse 90* was the only dramatic anthology that aired consistently, and by 1964 all were gone (Kraszewski 2010, 104). Boddy explains how the change affected television writers: "For many of the most prominent writers and critics in television, the move to the continuing character series was more than merely a shift in programs forms or commercial practices; it meant an end to their careers in the medium" (1993, 191).

In this context, ABC executive Daniel Melnick stated that the new action-adventure series that were appearing on television required "a different type of television writer, one who doesn't have a burning desire to make an original statement" (Boddy 1993, 197). But after enjoying the prestige of the "artist-playwright" with creative license, many writers resisted becoming little more than employees subject to the whims of sponsors or bottom-line network executives. Some returned to theater or shifted to screenwriting; others, such as Rod Serling and Leslie Stevens, formed independent production companies in order to maintain their autonomy in a changing television landscape. Serling formed his own company, Cayuga Productions, to create *The Twilight Zone* for CBS. In 1959, Stevens created Daystar Productions to make films free of studio interference. Like other "new entrepreneurs" who saw themselves as artists, Stevens resented the executives and money men who, according to Schow, handed down commercially motivated edicts that hampered his artistic expression. As Stevens stated, "Basically, I'm a writer. I became a director to protect the writer, and I became a producer to protect both of them, and a company owner to protect them all" (Schow 1998, 13). Stevens produced and directed his own films, albeit on a low budget. He stated, "When millions are involved, you have to satisfy the bankers. I want to satisfy myself. I don't need money now; I want freedom—and in the movies, you can only have freedom on a low budget" ("New Wavelet"). Even when Daystar moved into television, the company maintained its independence by partnering with United Artists, who gave Daystar financial backing but allowed Stevens and Stefano to maintain creative control. According to Alvey, the studio provided financing, studio space, postproduction facilities, and distribution, while Daystar provided concepts, hired talent, and coordinated production (1997, 145). This arrangement allowed Stevens and Stefano to make meaningful work in the guise of genre fiction.

Genre Television and "Low" Culture

Like the live dramatic anthologies, genres such as science fiction and horror were part of television since its inception; however, they rarely secured a prominent place on the schedule. Science fiction and horror—whether in books, comics, films, or television—were typically viewed as pulp entertainment targeted to juvenile or niche audiences. According to Howell, who argues that science fiction, horror, and fantasy were legitimated as "quality" television in the 1990s by paradoxically delegitimizing their generic characteristics, "The assumption is that science fiction is a non-artistic, highly commercial, formulaic television genre, juvenile in both content and audience, and achieving quality only through allegorical didacticism" (2017, 38). Televised science fiction was considered sensationalized "pulp" that entertained viewers through spectacle. Telotte notes, "Serials and series routinely brought to life the iconic characters and technologies that already dominated the covers of popular fiction—pulp magazines and futuristic novels—featuring spacecraft and flying platforms, death rays and reanimators, rocket packs and robots that had already captured the imaginations of their readers" (quoted in Miller 2012, 15). But *The Outer Limits* combined art and pulp, merging serious, thought-provoking social commentary with the familiar accoutrements of science fiction and horror. It conveyed an artistic vision without downplaying its associations with genre and in this way addressed "highbrow" viewers along with children and fans of science fiction. In the guise of escapist entertainment, it was simultaneously unnerving and provocative.

When television first became a staple of American homes in the late 1940s and early 1950s, there were three types of science fiction programs to choose from: those clearly aimed at youthful audiences, such as *Captain Video and His Space Rangers* (1949–55), *Captain Midnight* (1954–56), or *Tom Corbett, Space Cadet* (1950–55); adult-oriented science fiction programs aimed at niche audiences such as *Out There* (1951–52), *Tales of Tomorrow* (1951–53), and *Science Fiction Theatre*; and, less commonly, occasional science fiction-themed episodes on live dramatic anthology series. There were few shows oriented to horror even in the early days of television; *Lights Out* (1949–52) combined science fiction and horror, while two strictly horror programs were Roald Dahl's *Way Out* (1961), which lasted only six episodes, and *Thriller*

(1960–62), hosted by Boris Karloff. None of the genre programs aired during prime time, and, of those aimed at adults, only *Lights Out* lasted more than two seasons.

As was common in televised science fiction, programs drew from preexistent media. For example, *Captain Video*, which aired on Du-Mont at 7 p.m. in fifteen-minute installments three times a week, had been a film serial; *Tom Corbett* was based on a novel by Robert Heinlein; and both *Captain Midnight* and *Lights Out* began as radio programs in the 1930s. Similar to those aimed at children, the few adult-oriented science fiction series often adapted stories published by science fiction writers in pulp magazines. *Science Fiction Theatre* promised stories based on scientific fact, as did early publicity material for *The Outer Limits* (though, as noted in the introduction, the series diverged from this plan). Yaszek writes that while programs such as *Science Fiction Theater* were acclaimed by critics and viewers for their precise adaptations and fidelity to science, they were too narrow to appeal to prime-time audiences (2008, 57). She asserts that science fiction stories with more general appeal aired on dramatic anthology programs. These were developed from stories by writers such as Ray Bradbury and Judith Merril, who were known outside of the science fiction community; moreover, they fulfilled the dictates of "serious" rather than pulp science fiction—that "authors should create stories that put a human face on the sometimes overwhelmingly abstract problems attending dreadful new sciences and technologies" (Westfahl 1999, 184). According to Bould, the dramatic anthologies, "which tended to subjugate science to a blend of adventure, soap opera, topicality (sometimes even seriousness) and moralizing, largely established the parameters of American TV sf" (2003, 89). *The Outer Limits*, whose creators were more familiar with dramatic anthologies than science fiction, hewed to this model.

The Outer Limits was indebted to *Science Fiction Theater* in terms of its generic presentation and the way it was sold to ABC; to *Way Out* and *Thriller* in terms of its incorporation of Gothic horror; to "serious"   27 science fiction dramas that appeared on anthology series; and to its immediate predecessor, *The Twilight Zone. The Outer Limits* emulated these programs by combining science fiction and horror, adapting dramatic forms to television, and making social criticisms through allegory. In terms of the latter, Johnson-Smith describes both *The Twilight Zone* and *The Outer Limits* as "among the more daring shows of the era—in any genre—specifically because they grasped the potential for social commentary in television" (2005 58).

Merging Highbrow and Lowbrow

One of *The Outer Limits'* innovations was its combination of the highbrow aims and dramatic techniques of anthologies committed to social criticism and lowbrow genre fiction packaged for mass entertainment. In so doing, Stevens and Stefano's work demonstrates how writers and producers adapted to constraints on their creative autonomy in an industry concerned with profit and intent on avoiding controversial material. In this context, genre fiction served as a way to convey serious ideas in a context that otherwise discouraged such endeavors. According to Stefano, "I saw in *The Outer Limits* an opportunity to express the normal worries that a man with a wife and growing son in this country would have, and the censors didn't mind that, because whatever ideas were being expressed were all in the realm of fantasy, to them" (Schow 1998, 82). As Stefano recounted at a Paley Center forum in 2000, one of his worst problems with censors had to do with evolution. ABC did not want him to do any shows on the topic because the network did not want to offend southern affiliates; in the 1960s, many southern schools still did not teach evolution. Stefano's response, however, was "The Sixth Finger," an episode where a scientist conducts an experiment on a coal miner that enables him to evolve into a genius, after which he regresses back to an ape. The script was contentious, but, according to story editor Lou Morheim, "in the end we prevailed . . . the changes we were asked to make by ABC in the beginning were never made" (Schow 1998, 103).

In the midst of social change, a television program that questioned government, technology, and even what it means to be human stood out amid more prosaic television fare. According to associate producer Allan Balter, "We were crusaders; we were nuts trying to do television better than anyone else. . . . Leslie wasn't just a producer. He was a guy who wanted to make the world a better place" (Schow 1998, 17). In *The Outer Limits*, artistic, highbrow science fiction and horror provided an entry point to the show's social and political commentary and demonstrated that genre fiction could convey thought-provoking material to a broad audience. Together, both Stevens and Stefano, along with their production crew and the cadre of writers whose work they oversaw, conveyed the anxieties and potentialities of the modern age.

2

TELEVISUALITY IN *THE OUTER LIMITS*

Noir Science and Gothic Science Fiction

The Outer Limits was a product of television's transition from New York to Hollywood, from live to filmed programming, and from theatrical teleplays that addressed social and political issues to episodic series designed to avoid controversial content. In this context, *The Outer Limits* merged science fiction themes and imagery with the dramatic immediacy of theater and the cinematic conventions of film noir and Gothic horror in order to enhance its allegorical meaning. In so doing, it illuminated the interrelationship of film and television, which is often ignored in accounts of early television history. The series expanded the aesthetic possibilities of television and presaged the shift to televisuality in the 1980s and 1990s.

Televisuality in *The Outer Limits*

The television industry's move from New York to Hollywood, in addition to the switch from live to filmed programs, largely ended the debate about television as art intended to edify viewers vs. television as popular entertainment aimed at reaching the broadest possible segment of the public. The commercial imperative for television to be accessible and to appeal to mass audiences accounts for what Caldwell refers to as the "effacement of style" in early television programs; often "nondescript and cheaply made," telefilms produced on Hollywood sound stages replicated the familiar "zero-degree" Hollywood film style consisting of "generic establishing shots, shot-reverse shots, reaction shots, and cutaways" (1995, 51). As he asserts, popular television programs such as sitcoms or westerns eschewed excessive style; as a result, if their stories called for any kind of flourish, they typically "corralled expressive images into special narrative boxes as 'altered states'" (52).

While most episodic television was "zero-degree," there were some visually expressive offerings. In 1955, Hollywood studios began to sell "B" movies, such as science fiction and horror, to television. As Caldwell observes, "Cinema did not just import programs, it imported a way of seeing narrative and a distinctive way of seeing images" (1995, 50). This was particularly the case with science fiction and horror, which rely heavily on image and sound to create their effects. Although *The Outer Limits* was grounded in science fiction, it freely borrowed expressionist imagery from film noir and Gothic horror, employing what Prawer describes as the "film rhetoric of the macabre": techniques such as "slanted camera angles, filterings and blurrings, distortions through wide-angled lenses, low-key lighting, double exposures, accelerated or slowed-down or arrested motion, infrared film, sudden intrusions of film negatives, the use of colours or colour contrasts to convey mood, or shifts in scale" (1980, 29). Critic Jeff Shannon's tribute to *The Outer Limits'* cinematographer Conrad Hall aligns him with this rhetoric, writing that Hall "mastered the efficient use of shadow, negative space, oblique angles, and *noir*-influenced lighting effect to maximize the series' visual impact on a minimal TV budget" (2011). The fact that *The Outer Limits* was shot on 35 mm black-and-white film also gave it a cinematic look and lent it to expressionistic techniques suited to eliciting terror, fear, and suspense.

At the same time, *The Outer Limits* maintained its ties to the theatrical traditions of dramatic anthologies and remained subject to many of same constraints: episodes were typically shot on a KTTV soundstage on an MGM back lot, confined to a few sets with a limited cast of actors, and took place in continuous time. Yet these limitations allowed the show to incorporate the dramatic anthology's psychological realism and focus on character, while word, image, and sound worked together to create a visceral response.

Sound was also important to its rhetoric of the macabre. As Stefano states in "The Canons," "The mad magic of SOUND must be employed as often and as artfully as is feasible. The ear must never be a step-brother to the eye" (Schow 1998, 354). In her extensive analysis of music and sound effects in *The Outer Limits*, Wissner argues that they stimulate the viewer's imagination and provide "aural escapism" (2016). The combination of manual, vocal, and electronic instruments, whether invented for the show or recycled from other programs, enhance words and images and draw viewers into the story.

The Outer Limits illustrates how televisuality—a term that here encompasses both visual and aural techniques—emerges from theatrical and cinematic traditions and provides the foundation for *The Outer Limits* as a mode of television that works to "bring thrills and terrors into the home, giving expression to anxieties that were often related to those of the time" (Wheatley 2006, 38). This chapter first considers "Nightmare" as "noir science fiction" that merges science fiction and noir imagery, then focuses on "The Bellero Shield" as an example of "Gothic science fiction." Both "Nightmare" and "The Bellero Shield" blend theatrical and cinematic styles in order to create horror associated with misguided science and technology. At a time when most television eschewed excessive style and avoided overtly social and political commentary or thought-provoking material, *The Outer Limits* stood apart as a text that simultaneously unsettled and engaged viewers.

Noir Science Fiction in "Nightmare"

Because they are not constrained by the requirements of verisimili-tude, television genres such as science fiction and horror have always been freer to experiment than shows that aim for realism. Both John-son (2005) and Wheatley (2006) write that many television writers and producers in the 1950s and 1960s sought to overcome television's technical limitations through narrative and aesthetic experimen-tation, with TV horror at the vanguard of such efforts (Jowett and Abbot, 3). Science fiction and horror were given latitude because they were not taken seriously; as Howell writes, science fiction, horror and fantasy were considered low culture forms because of their lack of verisimilitude. She quotes Steven Neale: "The predominance of ide-ologies of realism in our culture tends to mean that, unless marked as high art, many avowedly non-realist genres are viewed as frivolously escapist, as 'mere fantasy,' and thus as suitable only for children or for 'mindless,' ''irresponsible' adults" (Howell 2017, 39).

While perceptions of science fiction and horror as mere escapist entertainment enabled Stevens and Stefano to make veiled social and political criticisms, their lack of a need for realist representation also freed them to transform television from a "window on the world" into a "window on the otherworldly" (Sconce 1997, 23). "Nightmare" is a prime example of the way *The Outer Limits* imaginatively combined theatrical and cinematic styles to make a powerful social statement through science fiction. The episode exemplifies what Ursini refers to as "noir science fiction": science fiction whose visual stylization re-flects the fear, paranoia, and sense of mystery characteristic of noir films; indeed, Ursini asserts that *The Outer Limits* was the most no-table noir science fiction television series of the 1960s (1999, 233). As is the case with classic film noir rooted in the American crime and detective fiction of the 1930s and 1940s, noir science fiction achieves its effects through a combination of visual style and thematic content. Low-key lighting and disorienting camera angles, deep focus shots, off-center placement of figures, distorted set design, and special effects all create the "nightmare" of the episode's title. Similarly, the episode illustrates another characteristic of noir style: "a dreamlike, surrealist atmosphere" where "characters seem to exist in a nocturnal world of shadow and menace that is almost identical to the horror film" (Meehan 2008, 5–6). As with film noir, formal techniques convey the pessimism, insecurity, and anxiety that characterized American society during the Depression, World War II, and the post–World War II era. While the emergence of film noir can be traced to American crime and detective fiction of the 1930s and 1940s, by the mid-1950s it had waned; as Schrader asserts, "as the rise of McCarthy and Eisenhower demonstrated, Americans were eager to see a more bourgeois view of themselves. . . . Any attempt at social criticism had to be cloaked in ludicrous affirmations of the American way of life. Technically, television, with its demand for full lighting and close-ups, gradually undercut the German influence, and color cinematography was, of course, the final blow to the noir look" (1972, 589). But *The Outer Limits* was an exception. As "noir science fiction," it combined the visual style and thematic underpinnings of film noir with science fiction to explore fears around the power of science and technology, particularity with regard to the specter of nuclear holocaust, extraterrestrial invasion, surveillance and the military-industrial complex, and the precariousness of individual autonomy and identity.

"Nightmare" (1963) addresses several of these noir science fiction themes. It begins in the future, in the midst of a war between Earth and the planet Ebon. There is very little plot: for the most part, the episode is structured as a prisoner's dilemma–like situation: the alien Ebonites capture a group of soldiers from Earth and subject them to physical or psychological torture designed to make each of them suspect the other of collaborating with the enemy. The soldiers become increasingly unraveled, and civilized behavior breaks down.

At first, the episode seems to be a simple Cold War allegory, with the Ebonites as stand-ins for Communists who purportedly used psychological techniques to brainwash American prisoners of war during World War II and the Korean War. Like many episodes of *The Outer Limits*, the story and structure of "Nightmare" draw from a previous source, in this case *The Purple Heart* (1944), a film—itself loosely based on a real incident—that depicted the Japanese military's interrogation, psychological manipulation, and torture of American POWs during World War II (Schow 2018). The brainwashed American who "turns red" was a common Cold War trope (Glover 2019, 125). It appeared in several films throughout the 1950s and 1960s, the best-known of which is *The Manchurian Candidate* (1962). Unlike World War II films that laud the heroic individual, both *The Manchurian Candidate* and "Nightmare" express anxiety about American vulnerability in the face of technology. At one point in "Nightmare," the American general states, "War isn't what it used to be—it's just computers and technical magic. You can't fight against brain work. You can't win."

Most important, "Nightmare's" narrative relies on noir iconography accompanied by disconcerting sounds for the power of its critique. It begins with stock footage of a missile striking earth, followed by an atomic explosion, an iconic image that immediately evokes fear of nuclear holocaust. The Control Voice explains that a "unified Earth" is at war with the planet Ebon. There is a cut to six men on what appears to be a spaceship; the frame is slightly akilter as their colonel warns, "Live or die, win or lose, we are going to remember at all times that we are human beings." Anxiety heightens after another explosion; the camera shakes, and the screen cuts to black. The sounds of a throbbing heartbeat punctuate the screams, followed by a matte image of the black planet Ebon.

After the expository opening, the entirety of the episode takes place on two sparsely decorated soundstages with the self-enclosed feel of a theatrical play: a claustrophobic compound where the soldiers are imprisoned by the Ebonites, and a cramped interrogation room. The compound is in a clearing set against a backdrop of rocks whose geometric shapes and angles create an abstract, other-worldly effect.

Silhouetted prisoners line up against the stark landscape of Ebon in "Nightmare."

As the men identify themselves, they form a line silhouetted against a blank background; then, one by one, each man is shot in close-up as he recites his name and rank, again against an entirely empty backdrop. There is no context; the effect is both surreal and beautiful.

Throughout the episode, the sparsity of the set is offset by startling visual and aural special effects. For example, when Private Dix, portrayed by Martin Sheen, attempts to escape, the Ebonites zap him with a wand. There is an extreme close-up of his mouth making no sound; spirals, accompanied by discordant sound effects, emanate from the wand and fill the screen, after which he loses the power of speech.

Spirals, a recurrent motif throughout the episode, are indicative of disintegration, in contrast to the wholeness implied by circular imagery. In yet another disturbing image later in the episode, Dix again tries to flee and runs into the void that is the landscape of Ebon (an effect created by a black velvet cloth as backdrop); an overhead crane

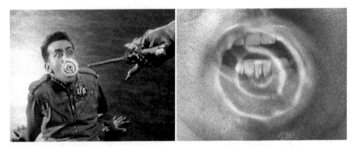

Spirals are a recurring motif in "Nightmare."

shot captures his mental breakdown as he screams and flails help-lessly, dwarfed by the emptiness that surrounds him.

Close-ups, long dialogue sequences, and the bare set focus atten-tion on the prisoners' fear, terror, and psychological disintegration as they face threats from within and without. The lack of an elaborate set design, while heightening the dramatic impact, also serves a prag-matic function: it is likely that the main costs were for the ensemble cast, which consisted of well-known performers (Ed Nelson, Martin Sheen, James Shigeta, Bill Gunn, and Sasha Harden). At a time when diversity on television was uncommon, the casting of an Asian actor (Shigeta) as Major Jong and an African American (Gunn) as Lieutenant Willomore is a visual way of portraying a "unified" Earth, though this unity is un-dercut when class and race differences become the basis of the men's suspicions. When the Ebonites take away and then restore Lieutenant Willomore's sight, Major Jong suggests that Willomore's race gave him a motive for talking to the Ebonites. Jong surmises, "Sight is a very precious thing, especially to a man who's had to endure the blindness of other people's minds." But the Asian Major Jong, identified as "other" through Eastern musical cues as well as his propensity to recite poetry, is the one the men accuse of being the traitor. According to Holcomb and Holcomb (2008b), Jong's love of poetry makes him "a subversive of the heart, a crime unto itself to the military minds who control the experiment."

Expressionist noir techniques are most obvious in the scenes that take place in the interrogation room. One by one the men are taken to a spare, dark cubicle where the Ebonites try to secure their cooperation. Canted camera angles and exaggerated shadows heighten the sense of unease. The Ebonites, who are able to read minds, induce hallucinations presented through special effects. Each of the men has a vision of a significant figure from their past, the images surrounded by a swirling ring of smoke. Camera position is also important: high-angle shots of the supposedly monstrous Ebonites place them in positions of power in contrast to low-angle shots of the vulnerable prisoners.

Moreover, extreme close-ups of the men's terrified faces as they face the Ebonites create a jarring rather than an intimate effect. As

The claustrophobic interrogation room of "Nightmare."

Rypel sums it up, "The stylization in 'Nightmare' is human drama played out against a *surreal* backdrop—human beings captured, terrorized, and tormented by nightmare creatures, the Ebonites, whose makeup suggests nothing so much as classical depictions of demons, lend the episode the unsettling atmosphere of a brief sojourn in hell" (1977, 52). On the episode's "subtle surrealism," Blamire writes, "Like much of *The Outer Limits* there is a strong sense of dreamscape, as though we're all prisoners of a tapped subconscious come to life. Visually, Ebon could almost be the creation of surrealist painter Yves Tanguy" (2011). The merging of noir and surrealist imagery will be explored further in chapter 4's discussion of "The Guests."

Rich sound and music compensate for the sparse set designs in "Nightmare" and intensify the eerie visual images. According to Holcomb and Holcomb (2008a), composer Dominic Frontiere gives *The Outer Limits* "an aural character perfectly harmonized with the emblematic thematic and visual style of the show." Here he uses a sonorous blend of instruments that alternates with discordant sound effects. In the interrogation scenes, for example, there is a "slow, queasy, monotonous bending-note whine" (Blamire 2011). The result is doubtless intended to unnerve and disorient viewers.

The ending, a condemnation of modern "war games" and instrumentalist science, supports *The Outer Limits'* overarching theme of humans as more monstrous than the monsters. The motif of playing games that runs through the episode is highlighted when, after the men decide that Jong is the traitor, they draw straws to see who will kill him. The twist comes when the Ebonites are shown observing the men along with a general from Earth, and the aliens protest that the "experiment" has gone too far. It turns out that the Earth's military forces, rather than the Ebonites, are the true aggressors. The Ebonites, who had accidentally struck Earth, are making amends by assisting the military with their "experiment" to see how much psychological torture the prisoners can endure before they break. When the general insists that the experiment needs to be seen through to its conclusion, one of the Ebonites protests and tries to save Jong's life. The soldiers turn on the Ebonite and attempt to kill him instead. The general (along with the prisoners' leader, Colonel Stone) intervenes, but in the ensuing scuffle is shot dead. There is no satisfying resolution; anxieties raised by the show's form and content are intensified rather than abated. Tellingly, while *The Purple Heart* ends with the Japanese military commander committing suicide when he realizes he cannot break the soldiers, "Nightmare" concludes with the confused and frightened prisoners murdering one of their own. Fear of the other is turned on its head; the evil is within, and the episode concludes not with a restoration of order that affirms human nature, but a descent into barbarity. Stefano has described his intentions in making the episode:

> I had some very strong problems with the government situation at that time. Space was not bad; space agencies were not bad. But I had little faith, and virtually no trust, in the people in charge of the Space Age. In World War II, the military dropped the Atom Bomb, and everyone thought that was great because it ended the war. If you wanted to give something the stamp of approval, you made it military, and I was attacking part of that faith in the military. (Schow 1998, 127)

"Nightmare" is not just a Cold War allegory; it is also a critique of the instrumentalist mindset of a government willing to deceive its citizens and sacrifice its soldiers. Even beyond its criticism of the military, the episode's condemnation of human nature shows how easily civilized behavior can degenerate into barbarity. It uses dramatic theatrical conventions to focus on characters and convey psychological realism in an otherwise unreal setting, while its use of noir science fiction builds tension and heightens anxiety.

"The Bellero Shield" as Gothic Science Fiction

"Nightmare" was characterized by a sparse set design, heavy styliza-tion, rejection of realism, and intense focus on characters. A scath-ing critique of instrumental rationality, it also commented on the fragility of civilized behavior. Episodes more explicitly structured as Gothic horror also explored the theme of the shadow side of human nature. Ledwon names three characteristics of the Gothic that apply to several episodes of *The Outer Limits*: (1) the use of standard Gothic devices which generally are recognized as capable of producing fear or dread; (2) the central enigma of the family; and (3) a difficult nar-rative structure that frustrates attempts at understanding (1993, 261). In a similar vein, Wheatley refers to Gothic television as the "un-derside" of television drama, both a narrative form that exploits the anxieties and terrors of family life, and a style characterized by a cer-tain "darkness or gloominess" (2006, 12). According to Cherry, who draws on Wheatley's work, "The Gothic mode on tv is one that draws on narrative and aesthetics in order to provide the emotional effects of terror, eliciting in the viewer the thrills and pleasures of a certain 'shiver-sensation'" (2014, 487). The "shiver-sensation" is what Stefano refers to as the BEAR in "The Canons," and what is induced by the monsters and aliens in science fiction. Indeed, several episodes of *The Outer Limits* merge a concern with the relationship between hu-mans and technology that is characteristic of science fiction and the experience of terror associated with horror and may therefore be characterized as Gothic science fiction.

"The Bellero Shield" is a representative episode of *The Outer Lim-its* that demonstrates how Gothic science fiction brings fear and terror into the home. It was written and produced by Stefano, filmed by Conrad Hall, and directed by John Brahm, whom film historian Andrew Sarris cited for his "mood-drenched melodramas" in the 1930s (1985, 263). Its complex exploration of gender, ambition, and power combines the theatricality and expressionism of "Nightmare" with the warnings about technology that abound in science fiction. The episode, which takes place entirely inside the Bellero home, illustrates Wheatley's observation that the Gothic is "the most domestic of genres on the most domestic of media" (2006, 12). In a postwar milieu marked by conventional gender roles where the "ideal" wife was confined to the home, the episode speaks to the domestic containment of women in the Cold War era. May writes, "The home contained not only sex, consumer goods, children, and intimacy, but enormous discontent, especially for women. For many, there was no place else for this discontent to go, so it remained contained in the home" (1999, 207). "The Bellero Shield" is a literal metaphor for domestic containment that works on multiple levels. At the heart is trauma around the family, conveyed in a manner that follows Stefano's story requirement that "each play must reveal something of the inner life of man" (Schow 1998, 354). As such, the episode serves as a condemnation of the way the sins of ruthless ambition and greed corrupt humankind. In an episode rife with religious allusions, humans encounter through scientific exploration a godlike being but try to exploit it for earthly gain.

"The Bellero Shield" uses Gothic tropes and motifs to create a shiver-inducing atmosphere of dread. *The Outer Limits* typically began with a dramatic cold open drawn from the middle of the episode: as an anthology, it did not have the benefit of continuing characters or a familiar formula, and so ABC insisted on a teaser scene to draw viewers into the narrative. The teaser often revealed the climax of the episode, as was the case here. It displays several hallmarks of the Gothic: rather than a conventional establishing shot, the shows begins with a medium wide-angle shot of a tomb-like wine cellar. In the corner of the frame a small dark female figure dressed in black drags a glowing yet barely discernible body toward a corner of the cellar.

Discordant electronic chords provide an unsettling aural accompaniment. Chiaroscuro lighting creates exaggerated shadows and conceals more than it reveals. As the woman begins to ascend the

"The Bellero Shield" opens in a tomb-like cellar.

stairs, the camera cuts to a medium close-up in which she is visually imprisoned, caught between the staircase spindles on the right and their heightened shadows on the left. The music intensifies as she hears a sound, and a man is framed by the doorway at the top of the stairs, filmed at an exaggerated high angle followed by a low-angle reverse shot from where the woman stands at the bottom of the stairs. The camera follows her as she advances toward him. Both meet near the top of the stairs, and the woman intones, "There is a bullet at the base of his skull," before informing the man that she is going to bury the body. In what Schow refers to as "the lustiest, most arch-Shakespearian line of the episode," he replies, "My son didn't do it. Great men are *forgiven* their murderous wives" (1998, 187). In

response, she moves to slap him, and he loses his balance and hurtles downward, going out of frame so that only his cry is heard as he falls to his death. The camera then follows the woman again as she slowly descends the stairs to where his body lies next to the glowing white creature she tried to hide. The special effects are crude: actor John Hoyt, who plays the alien, is dressed in a white bodysuit, wears a featureless white mask, and is filmed through a Vaseline-coated pane of glass held in front of the camera lens through which light is reflected to create a shimmering, blurry effect (Schow 1998, 188). Shot in a close-up, the creature opens its eyes and moves its mouth. Realizing it is not dead, the woman gasps and opens her mouth to scream, but no sound comes out. She freezes and holds her hand up to her mouth, gazing upward as the camera zooms in to her face to emphasize her terror.

Throughout the episode, the play of light and dark is both literal and metaphorical. The purposefully obscure opening lures viewers into the narrative, and the combined effects build suspense and establish an ominous mood and tone that is decidedly "unhomey." In so doing, "The Bellero Shield" distinguishes itself from episodic television programs where home, often represented by a kitchen or living room, is a site of solace and comfort; instead, the home is introduced as a site of fear and danger, located within the realm of the uncanny rather than the familiar. It is signified not by communal spaces, but by the Gothic trope of the cellar, a cold and claustrophobic place not typically visible that in this case hides murderous secrets.

After the opening teaser and a brief break for ads, the credit sequence leads into an establishing shot of a desolate mansion. Like the "haunted houses" of many Gothic tales, it is isolated from the outside world, though white beams of light pulse from the roof to the sky. Inside, the beams are accounted for by a scientist operating a lab full of whizzing dials and complicated machinery, well-known signifiers from science fiction. He is accompanied by an older man, seated in the foreground. The Control Voice then introduces the theme of the episode: "There is a passion in the human heart which is called aspiration . . . and by its light man has traveled from the caves of darkness to the darkness of outer space." There is a cut to a woman dressed in a floor-length white gown pacing back and forth in a dimly lit room. The Control Voice continues, "But when this passion becomes lust, when its flame is fanned by greed and private hunger, then aspiration becomes ambition." Another cut shows a close-up of a woman's bare feet and contrasting black dress, then cuts back to the first woman in center frame, who is smiling as the Control Voice ends ominously, "By which sin the angels fell." The teleplay, written by Stefano with Lou Morheim, describes the woman as follows: "There is a soft, withdrawn quality about her, a reserve that can easily be mistaken for gentleness, even tenderness, but which is, in reality, an artful and studied mask for passionate, consuming ambition."

As Schow observes, "'The Bellero Shield' combines Shakespeare with ancient mythology, pulp science fiction, quasi-religious overtones, and legitimate theatre via it its 'perfect number' cast of five and the stagey, embroidered quality of the performance" (1998, 183–84). As in a theatrical play, there is a limited cast and few settings: the action all takes place in one evening, and the majority of scenes occur in three locations—Richard Bellero's lab, the pantry, and the wine cellar. As was the case with the depiction of the planet Ebon in "Nightmare," an artificial, "otherworldly" quality facilitates an allegorical reading.

The story develops through sequences of two-person scenes that build to its chilling ending. Judith Bellero, powerless in the patriarchal world she inhabits, dreams of attaining fame through her husband Richard (Martin Landau). There is a doubling motif characteristic of many Gothic stories: the tall, blonde, and patrician Judith (Sally Kellerman) is paired with her housekeeper, the small, dark, and mysterious Mrs. Dame (Chita Rivera). Mrs. Dame's stark, high-necked black housecoat and bare feet—indicating stealth—contrast with Judith's luxurious white velvet gown with its fur-lined collar. Familiar to Gothic fiction, Mrs. Dame is a sinister figure, who carries a gun that she once used to kill her abusive husband; symbolically, she hands it

46

off to Judith early in the episode. The only other characters are Bellero Sr., Richard's father (Neil Hamilton), who despises Judith and refuses to let Richard inherit his company unless he leaves her, and an alien creature who is accidentally drawn into the Bellero home by one of Richard's inventions.

Stefano drew inspiration for "The Bellero Shield" from a short science fiction story, "The Lanson Screen," (1936) written by Arthur Leo Zagat and published in a pulp magazine, *Thrilling Wonder Stories*. In it, a scientist invents a force field to protect Manhattan, but dies before finding a way to deactivate it. Stefano injects drama into the story by giving it a "haircut": his term for casting classic stories, in this case *Macbeth*, as science fiction. But what distinguishes "The Bellero Shield" as Gothic science fiction is the confluence of home and scientific laboratory as sites of terror, communicated through dialogue, images, and music working together to give allegorical expression to contemporary anxieties. As Ledwon observes, "The domestic gone horribly wrong is the essence of the Television Gothic . . . Better the Gothic than the horror of everyday domestic life" (1993, 264). But "The Bellero Shield" also demonstrates technology gone horribly wrong—a dominant theme in science fiction. Wasson and Alder write, "The Gothic mode is often employed in science fiction preoccupied with the threatening nature of technology" (2011, 10). In this case, misguided scientific endeavor turns to horror.

As the narrative unfolds, Richard invents a laser gun that he and Judith hope will impress his father enough to make Richard heir to his company. As Judith, accompanied by Mrs. Dane, secures a bottle of champagne from the cellar in preparation for their celebration, the soundtrack is silent, the quiet emphasized by a close-up of Mrs. Dane's bare feet descending the stairs. The cellar is dark and gloomy, filmed with imposing shadows, as Mrs. Dane blows dust from the bottle she removes from the shelf. The near-silence is followed by a discordant electronic vibration as Judith enters Richard's lab, a scene shot in odd angles with chiaroscuro lighting, as his father is leaving. The eerie music continues as Richard tells Judith that his father has no interest in a weapon of war and will not give him the company. The episode then demonstrates the subtle use of musical cues that make *The Outer Limits* so exemplary. Judith responds to Richard's news by professing her love, along with acknowledging her ambitions for him. A close-up portrays their silhouetted faces as they kiss passionately. The musical cue is a love theme that, according to Wissner, conforms to the stereotype of the virtuous wife: "Ascending, lyrical, diatonic melodies with even note values" (2016, 117). However, Wissner adds, this is an aural illusion. While the feigned love theme signals that Judith is a loving wife, this is belied not only by what viewers already know, but by the discordant electronic chord that continues to vibrate in the background. Despite their disappointment, Judith proposes a toast and bids Richard to get the crystal wine glasses. Her fury is made apparent when she attempts to smash the champagne bottle (inexplicably it remains intact) and then shoots at it with Richard's laser gun. Their marital dynamic is articulated by a visually complex scene shot through the refracted glass of the goblets that Mrs. Dame is polishing; Richard stands dejectedly in the dark, narrow pantry and asks her if Judith has ever talked about leaving him. "For what?" Mrs. Dame replies, an acknowledgment of Judith's limited options rather than a confirmation of her love.

After Judith fires the laser, a wailing, screeching sound begins and becomes louder as the beam pulses and a creature gradually materializes, unwillingly pulled into the lab by the ray that reaches into the sky.

Shocked and terrified, Judith shoots it with the laser gun and flees to tell Richard. When they return, the creature, an alien being made of solidified light, is unharmed. When the alien speaks, it demonstrates the show's use of sound to delineate character. In Stefano's script, the voice is described as "slow, liquid-beautiful, reverberates with its own mellow, self-enclosed echoes. It sounds distant, but not muffled." According to Murray, "The ingenious use of sound gives a truly alien feel

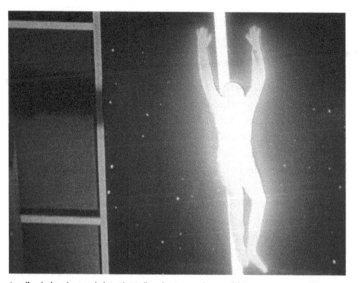

An alien being descends into the Bellero home on a beam of light.

to the creature's vocal quality. The contrast of the thing's soothing melodic voice and the tonal ringing hum at the beginning of every speech gives a truly outre feeling to this being" (1987, 30).

The incandescent alien contrasts with the dark Gothic household whose heavy curtains block out sunlight and project shadows; his gentle demeanor codes him as Christ-like, though Judith tellingly describes the being to Richard as "cold" and "chilling." The alien explains that it has protected itself with a shield that no weapons can penetrate, though it deactivates the shield when it realizes that it is safe. Judith tells Richard that the shield is their "Bifrost," the bridge in Norse mythology that connects Earth and the heavens; she believes that it will propel Richard to power and glory. She names it the Bellero Shield (notably, after her husband) and implores Richard to take it from the alien and convince his father that it is his own invention. She   49 becomes frustrated when Richard refuses and approaches the alien herself. When the alien tells her that it plans to leave, she asks it to wait "a minute" for Richard. In an example of the script's ornate theatrical language, the alien asks Judith how long a minute is, to which she replies in a manner that reveals her unhappiness: "It passes unnoticed, when you're content. For the needy, it can be a string of endless lifetimes." Judith, like many housewives in the 1950s and 1960s, is trapped in the patriarchal order, though she attempts to realize her ambitions by manipulating her husband.

Judith shoots the unprotected alien with Mrs. Dame's gun and disconnects the control device from its hand. Mrs. Dame, now her accomplice, hides the body in the cellar. In this, Stefano was influenced by Henri-Georges Clouzot's film *Les Diaboliques* (1955), where two women commit a murder and encounter difficulty disposing of the body (Schow 1998, 187). Both the film and the episode rely on tropes of film noir: a weak man, a femme fatale, and a crime that spirals out of control. (*Les Diaboliques* and its relationship to another Stefano episode, "Forms of Things Unknown," is discussed in chapter 4.) As in film noir, the transgressive—here overly ambitious—woman is punished; as in science fiction, the scientist who meddles in what he does not understand is similarly undone.

While conventional television programs reassured viewers with upbeat endings that primed them for the commercials, the opposite occurs here. When Judith summons Bellero Sr. back to the house to demonstrate how Richard's Bellero Shield operates, she encloses herself within it and asks Mrs. Dame to shoot her. After bullets from her handgun bounce off the shield, Judith suggests they try Richard's laser gun. Unable to restrain himself, Bellero Sr. grabs it from Mrs. Dame and fires; predictably, the rays bounce off the shield's wall. But when Judith attempts to deactivate the shield, she realizes that the alien never told her how. The visual image recalls *Macbeth*: when Judith presses on the glass, a translucent spot is visible on the palm of her hand that was left when she snatched the control device from the alien. An eerie glow of light—the alien's lifeblood—symbolizes her guilt. The shield, an effect created by a piece of plexiglass, allows for a number of complex shots as different characters are refracted when they interact with Judith. After all efforts to deactivate the shield fail, she confesses to the crime. The opening teaser is replayed: Bellero Sr. goes to the basement to find the alien's body, which he believes he will be able to parlay as proof of Richard's achievement while also allowing him to blame Judith for the murder, and he is accidentally killed by Mrs. Dame when she strikes at him and he falls down the stairs.

The final scene is one of the most disturbing endings of any episode in the entire series, one that offers a complication rather than a resolution and refuses to provide viewers the pleasure of narrative closure. Mrs. Dame realizes the alien is still alive and asks it to help

As Judith (Sally Kellerman) presses on the wall of the "Bellero Shield," it appears that she is pressing on the television screen itself.

Judith. "How can I not?" it replies, a not-so-subtle Christ allusion. The alien is "resurrected" and helps Judith by deactivating the shield before it dies. Judith presses on the nonexistent glass of the no-longer-operative shield, but she is still contained within its imaginary walls. There is no longer a physical barrier, but she remains trapped in a psychological prison of her own making.

"The Bellero Shield" creates an atmosphere of unremitting fear and dread that builds to its conclusion. On the narrative level, it produces what Stefano refers to as "tolerable terror": "When the play is ended, when the Control Voice has returned to the viewer the use of his [*sic*] television set, the viewer, that willing victim of the terror, must be able to relax and know self-amusement and realize that what he feared during the telling of the story could not materialize and need not be feared should he walk out of his house and stroll a night street" (Schow 1998, 354). But the social and political import of "The Bellero Shield" is conveyed through Gothic science fiction codes and conventions, rather than literal meaning. Through its allegory, "The Bellero Shield" allows fear to linger and provokes thought. Its perspective is dire; in the end, lust for power triumphs over goodness and culminates in death and madness. The closing narration makes clear that humans, rather than the alien, are "fallen angels": the Control Voice repeats the opening line, "When this passion called aspiration becomes lust . . . then aspiration degenerates . . . becomes vulgar ambition, by which sin the angels fell."

The philosophical rumination on human nature is grounded by the Gothic, whose narrative and stylistic strategies express anxieties around the instability of the family and conventional gender roles. Sconce discusses the social implications of the chilling final scene that breaks the fourth wall:

> Close-ups of the entombed woman create the impression that the woman is actually pressing upon the viewer's home screen. The dynamic image of a woman flailing behind glass

walls, at first real and then imaginary, is a dense and multivalent emblem that merges the period's visions of electronic and domestic oblivion. Women like Judith were trapped by television in two ways, physically removed from the world and isolated from the world by its imperious domestic technology, while also trapped within its constricting conventions of representation. (1997, 35)

For many women in the 1950s and early 1960s, this suffocating image was all too real, made all the more terrifying by the "screen" that both protects and contains Judith within domestic space. "The Bellero Shield," while ostensibly a story about greed and ambition that conveys a "tolerable terror," comments on the constricting nature of representations that reinforce patriarchal authority and deny female agency, encapsulated by the image of the entrapped woman pressing on an imaginary screen. Yet, while Judith's behavior is explained by the restricting demands of a patriarchal order that conflicts with her desire, the episode undercuts its own feminist message. She functions as what Stefano refers to as the BEAR: Judith, rather than the alien, is the monster. Like Lady Macbeth, her lust for power drives her to murder and leads to madness. Like Lady Macbeth—and like the femme fatale of film noir—Judith is punished for her "unfeminine" ambition.

Long before the medium of television was considered "televisual," *The Outer Limits* merged theatrical and cinematic traditions to create episodes where word, sound, and image held equal import. Through its use of formal techniques, *The Outer Limits* disrupted a passive viewing experience and addressed contemporary anxieties. Noir science and Gothic science fiction revealed the "underside" of episodic television, technology, and postwar culture.

3
BEHIND THE NEW FRONTIER

In their introduction to *American Science Fiction*, Link and Canavan write, "Since WWI science fiction has been the genre of choice for authors who wanted the narrative freedom to explore new ideas and philosophies in compelling, challenging, and provocative ways" (2015, 10). They add, "SF has also—as an intellectual and artistic endeavor—been a major source of socioeconomic, political, and cultural critique" (10). *The Outer Limits* is no exception, and in chapter 3 I relate it to the Cold War tensions of the 1950s as they transition into the New Frontier of the 1960s. In the guise of entertaining genre fiction that is not "realistic," *The Outer Limits* relies on allegory and indirection to comment on contemporary issues. At the same time, it addresses themes central to science fiction concerning the relationship between humans and technology and the "nature" of human nature. While in chapter 2 I discussed how formal techniques provoked rather than reassured viewers, here I consider three representative episodes that convey how the themes of *The Outer Limits* provide critical commentary: "The Galaxy Being," "OBIT," and "Architects of Fear."

From the Cold War to the New Frontier

In the immediate aftermath of World War II, the United States and the Soviet Union pledged to cooperate with one another, though their agreement quickly dissolved when the Soviets installed Communist governments in Eastern Europe. In response, the United States established the Truman Doctrine in 1947, to contain the spread of Communism with a strong military presence around the world, along with technological advances and the build-up of nuclear arms to assure American dominance. Tensions were exacerbated when the Soviet Union also became a nuclear superpower in 1949; for the first time in history, two adversaries had weapons that could destroy the planet. Through the 1950s, this period was characterized by the rise of the military-industrial complex along with fear of its power, as evidenced by President Eisenhower's famous warning about its growing influence in his 1961 farewell address. In terms of family life, the domestic containment of women on the home front (discussed in chapter 2) functioned as the corollary of the foreign policy of containing Communism. The patriarchal nuclear family, by restoring male authority and confining women to the domestic sphere, would produce strong men ready and able to defend American values and "stand up to the Communists" (May 1999, 97).

Fear of Communism was directed both internally and externally, as evidenced by the House Un-American Activities Committee (HUAC), initially established in 1947 to determine the extent of Communist influence in American society. Three years later, the right-wing journal *Counterattack* released "Red Channels: The Report of Communist Influence in Radio and Television," which produced a list of "subversives" working in the entertainment industries. For the most part, these "subversives" were merely people with liberal politics, but in the atmosphere of anti-Communist fear and paranoia, and given the industry's desire to avoid controversy, those accused of being Communist sympathizers were blacklisted from working in television and film through the 1950s and into the 1960s. It's also noteworthy that, as Cochran points out, HUAC "did not just work to ferret out communists, but often also to squelch any perceived criticism of capitalism" (2010, 2). He states, "Clearly, the purpose of this policy of censorship was to repress the darker aspects of American social thought—the strong sense of doubt and contingency, the fears born of World War II, the atomic bomb, the Cold War—and replace them with a much more affirmative vision" (13).

This affirmative vision of America was conveyed through the idea of progress. The post–World War II period was marked by advances in electronics, such as the development of television, as well as the emergence of satellites, computers, and rocket technology that allowed for space exploration. Products and technologies developed for wartime purposes were adapted for commercial use, so a proliferation of consumer goods provided the economic engine of postwar prosperity. But by the end of the 1950s, the promise of America's technological and economic supremacy had given way to a series of disillusionments. Spigel remarks:

> The utopian dreams for technological supremacy, consumer prosperity, and domestic bliss were revealing their limits in ways that could no longer be brushed aside. With consumer debt mounting, the stock market felt its first major slide in 1957. In the same year, Americans witnessed the most stunning technological embarrassment of the times when the Soviet Union beat the United States into space with Sputnik. (1991, 108–9)

Kennedy's 1960 inaugural address introduced the "New Frontier," a policy based on space exploration and scientific innovation as a means to revitalize the economy, restore confidence in American technological supremacy, and allay fears of Soviet dominance in the aftermath of Sputnik. Spigel observes that the goals of the Kennedy administration merged particularly well with the television industry's need to fulfill its early promise as a medium that would edify viewers (1991, 114). By 1960, critics had become increasingly vocal in their complaints about vapid television programs. In 1961, FCC chairman

Newton Minow joined the chorus with his famous "vast wasteland" speech that condemned the medium for providing a plethora of escapist entertainment with little cultural value. The television industry, fearing regulation, seized on coverage of space exploration as one means of demonstrating a commitment to inform and educate viewers. Yet, as Troyan observes, "behind the Kennedy optimism promoted by magazines such as *Life* and televised space shots lay the shadow of the Cold War, the arms race, and the possibility of nuclear annihilation" (1993, 63). But in a context where ideas that discomforted viewers were not countenanced, most television fiction continued to provide upbeat, escapist entertainment. *The Outer Limits* was an exception that marked the return of the repressed.

"The Galaxy Being"

"The Galaxy Being" (like the series, originally titled "Please Stand By") was the pilot of *The Outer Limits*, produced, written, and directed by Stevens. In contrast to Stefano's Gothic science fiction (discussed in chapter 2), the episode adheres to the conventions of science fiction in its depiction of scientific "tinkering" gone awry. It features several hallmarks of the series: an intellectually curious scientist or inventor, misguided attempts to master technology get out of control, and an unsettling ending (Troyan 1993, 65). The "scientist" here is Allan Maxwell (played by Oscar winner Cliff Robertson), an amateur inventor who owns a radio station. Rather than attending to business, he spends his time in an adjacent transmission shed, working on a three-dimensional scanner he has built by illegally rerouting power from the radio station. Viewers are first introduced to him in his makeshift laboratory as he attends to a monitor that emits beeps and signals. Science fiction film and television often depict devices such as scanners, monitors, or screens that self-reflexively call attention to the medium (Telotte 2012, xvii). In this case, "The Galaxy Being" encourages viewers to relate form and content: on the monitor's screen is a sine wave, cleverly evoking the show's opening credits

Sine wave on Allan Maxwell's (Cliff Robertson) monitor mimics *The Outer Limits'* opening credits in "The Galaxy Being."

and linking the idea of losing control of television transmission to the episode that will ensue.

When Allan's wife, Carol (Jacqueline Scott), phones him from next door, he excitedly invites her to join him. His brother Gene (Lee Phillips), who co-owns the radio station, derisively comments, "He probably picked up a program from Telstar." The mention of Telstar, the first communications satellite launched in 1962, links television, space, and technology. As Sconce notes, "A symbol of the earth united through the heavens, the launching of Telstar strengthened an already strong cultural association between television and outer space, and reinvigorated television's status as an extraordinary and fantastic technology" (1997, 28). But Carol's reaction to the static that appears on Allan's monitor—"It puts my teeth on edge"—expresses fear rather than wonder. When the image begins to solidify, she   59 adds, "I don't like it. Don't ask me to appreciate it because I can't. It's cold. It sounds like sleet and snow and it looks like electricity, frozen"—a response that echoes that of Judith when she first meets the alien in "The Bellero Shield." Carol challenges Allan by pointing out that there are "experts" working on scientific discoveries, though it's worth noting that in many *Outer Limits* episodes, the "experts" are as misguided as the amateurs. Allan defends his work, claiming that most of the world's great inventions have been discovered by passionate "nobodies" like him. As Troyan writes, "The dream of eliminating distance, regaining mastery of individual activity and the belief in the inevitable upward swirl of technology and social progress are brought together in Allan's figure" (1993, 65). Allan's fascination with technology and desire for mastery comes at the expense of his marital relationship, made explicit when Carol concludes, "Well, I'm sorry, Allan but I don't like it. Because every day it takes you away from me more and more until I hardly know you." As the episode unfolds, we see that Allan's faith in technology is not only destroying his marriage and livelihood, but it is misplaced. Though science and technology may offer opportunities for uplift and discovery, they also have the potential for risk, danger, and death (Schow 1998, 36).

A ghostly visage forms out of the static on his screen, and the show's title, "The Galaxy Being," appears for the first time. According to Rypel, "It is a rational, extraterrestrial life force, an intelligent *being* we see, a being whose intellectual superiority to humankind is evinced by the consistently dominant angle at which it appears on camera; it looks *down* at the awestruck human whose electronic tinkering has contacted it across the void of space" (1977, 10). Allan's conversation with the alien is indicative of *The Outer Limits'* philosophical bent and illustrates the show's orientation to adult viewers as much as to youth. Allan asks two questions: "What is death?" and "Is there a God?"—both of which seem the stuff of nightmares for young viewers. Yet, despite contacting extraterrestrial life, Allan acquiesces to Carol's demand to attend a banquet being given in his honor (likely because she threatens to invite the attendees into his workspace). Rypel notes the irony and comments, "Mankind's stubborn pomposity—the nature of the honor bestowed on Maxwell is never related, but what could be more important than his present endeavor?—ultimately costs the loss of untold knowledge" (1977, 12).

Allan orders the evening's substitute deejay not to boost the power. The deejay disregards him and turns up the signal, causing the alien to materialize and emerge from the screen. In a startling visual effect, the viewer's television screen and the screen of Allan's monitor become indistinguishable, so that the alien appears to be coming out of the television and into the viewer's home.

Moreover, the technique used to create the alien, who appears to emit radiation waves, was especially inventive. A brown wet suit and mask was covered with oil and glycerin to reflect the lighting on the interior set, after which the film stock was negatively reversed so the costume became luminescent white. Because of this optical technique, the alien could not be filmed with any of the other characters, and its scenes had to be edited into the unaltered footage in postproduction (Schow 1998, 37). The effect is frightening and eerie.

The ensuing scene depicts the repercussions of technology run amok. The alien unintentionally destroys the radio station and kills

A creature appears on the monitor in "The Galaxy Being;" later it materializes and breaks out of the frame of the monitor screen.

the deejay, wreaking havoc afterward as it searches for Allan. The episode, clearly a variation on *Frankenstein*, similarly combines science fiction and horror in what Tudor refers to as a "knowledge narrative": scientific meddling gives rise to a threat to the ordered world of the known, which leads to a period of rampage, after which attempts are made to resist the threat, either through the application of expertise or coercion (1989, 81–83). In this case, the army is called in as Allan, carrying an unconscious Carol, who has been injured in the melee, takes the alien back to his lab to repair the monitor so that the alien can escape. The alien appears inside, but he tells Allan that it is too late. He has broken his race's laws, so they will destroy him. Both Allan and the alien face the repercussions of their unsanctioned explorations.

When Carol awakens and attempts to leave, the army mistakenly shoots her. The benign alien heals her, underscoring the folly of perceiving a being with the ability to aid humankind as a threat that must be destroyed. Rypel summarizes, "Man is depicted as a tiny, fragile creature, preoccupied with his self-importance; armed with important tools, yet lacking in wisdom" (1977, 10). The episode suggests that humankind—whether represented by Allan, the unruly mob gathered outside the radio station, or the army—lacks the ability to understand or control the technologies they have created, whether it be Allan's monitor, Telstar, or the television set. The alien underscores this message as he delivers a final message to the crowd assembled outside: "You people of this planet—you must not use force. . . . There is much you have to learn. You must explore. You must reach out. Go to your homes. Go and give thought to the mysteries of the universe." While Tudor writes that most often in knowledge narratives the monster is destroyed and order is restored, here the restoration of order is far more ambiguous (1989, 84).

There is yet another interpretation. In 1963, television was still new and unsettling, itself an "alien" technology. Sconce has suggested
that *The Outer Limits* maximized television's potential for horror by

playing on fears of the medium as an electronic void that threatened to assimilate viewers (1997, 23). It is telling in this regard that *The Outer Limits*' opening credits, and the images on Allan's monitor, portray television static, which Carol perceives as chilling and "otherworldly." According to Horrocks, "The classic motif of television in horror is the screen's rendition of 'dead time,' the image of electronic snow accompanied by the sound of static after the station has shut down for the night, before some unscheduled programming of an unearthly kind" (2017, 114). As seen in "The Galaxy Being," television serves as a portal to the "other side." Sconce recounts how, in popular lore of the 1950s, stories circulated of people trapped in an alternate reality behind the television screen, or even of the dead who existed in the television netherworld. While television was commonly perceived as a window on the world, "The Galaxy Being" stoked the fear that things outside the window could reach in and pull viewers into the electronic void. Sconce remarks, "Whether faced with new beings, mysterious powers, or strange technologies, the characters in these stories (and the viewer at home) had to struggle against uncanny and frequently electronic forces that threatened not just to kill them, but to dissolve them into nothingness" (1997, 24). Here we see just that with the unfortunate alien who tunes himself out of existence. He declares, "End of transmission," and disappears, merging into the oblivion of both outer space and the electronic void of television. In the closing narration the Control Voice promises to return control of the television set to viewers, though the entire episode is a reminder of how little control they have.

"OBIT"

"OBIT"—short for Outer Band Individuated Tracer—adds anxieties about loss of privacy and surveillance to those about space exploration and the power of television. OBIT is a secret surveillance machine created by the government to monitor individuals without their knowledge. According to Schow, the story was based on a book

63

Joseph Stefano read before passing on the idea to writer Meyer Dolinsky (1998, 118). The idea was similar to Isaac Asimov's *The Dead Past* (1956). Like "OBIT," it features a video screen where people observe one another and similarly addresses the invasion of privacy and people's obsession with watching others. Dolinsky, in turn, conceived of "OBIT" as a critique of HUAC; notably, the actor Jeff Corey, who plays the alien villain Lomax, had been blacklisted until 1960. According to Dolinsky:

> I'm very much in love with freedom. But I'm also concerned that we do have restraints against extreme totalitarianism. The political focus of OBIT is all mine; it's a reverse on the HUAC thing. These people, far from helping a free society, are really its worst enemy, in the sense they breed so much hostility and fear that they curiously accomplish the very thing they are trying to prevent. Witch-hunting is the wrong way to go about it. (Schow 1998, 117–18)

"OBIT" creates an atmosphere of fear and paranoia reminiscent of Communist "witch-hunting." It also reflects wariness of what Wildemuth refers to as the security state apparatus of the post–World War II era: "A surveillance culture that uses all forms of information technology, from print to electronics, to watch out for internal and external threats in the name of securing the safety of its citizenry" (2014, 3). The episode depicts an alliance between the government, the military, and scientists, who keep the existence of OBIT a secret; at the same time, it remains grounded in science fiction through its invasion narrative, where aliens disguised as humans have created the machines in order to weaken humankind so that they can take over. Stylistically, "OBIT" is a variation of noir science fiction that combines conventions from science fiction, film noir, and the courtroom crime genre. The result is aptly described by the term "tech noir": "Fiction that explores the dark side of human nature and how it interfaces with technology" (Meehan 2008, 13).

The episode opens with a high-angle crane shot of a lab so that viewers can watch the action from a distance. The camera cuts to a security officer who observes someone on a round screen. Suddenly, the blurry mage crystallizes into a one-eyed monster. On-screen, the monster's hands grasp the air, while off-screen, the image is echoed by human hands that press on his neck. Viewers watch the man as he watches himself being strangled by the monster, a self-reflexive moment that calls attention to the process of viewing.

The Control Voice explains what viewers have seen, stating, "Security personnel use OBIT to keep constant watch on the scientists at the Cypress Hills Research Center." The Voice further confides, "And so it would have remained except for the facts you are about to witness." In an episode that is all about people observing other people, viewers are immediately made complicit in watching.

The episode is structured as a courtroom drama in which US senator Orville (Peter Breck) investigates the murder that opens the episode. He calls to the stand witnesses who describe a culture of spying that has destroyed morale, which is easy to extrapolate to HUAC and the treatment of suspected Communists. One witness, who was

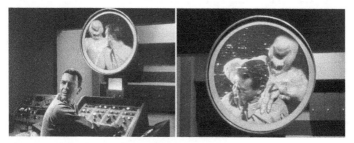

Viewers watch a man watch himself being strangled in "OBIT."

arrested by military police for expressing "problematic" ideas in a private letter, sounds the alarm that people "whisper in their own houses" and have to watch what they say, "even in their sleep." The researcher in charge of the OBIT machine, Dr. Lomax, explains their paranoia to Orville by revealing that because the "Peeping Tom" machine is secret, no one knows how their behavior is being monitored—only that it is. When Orville protests the invasion of privacy, Lomax parrots HUAC's rationalization for interrogating suspected Communists: "People with nothing to hide have nothing to fear."

When another member of the military command, Colonel Grover, is called to the stand, he reveals that hundreds of OBIT machines are being used at defense installations, in private industry, in education, and in communication networks. He warns that privacy is being made obsolete by the authorities who are supposed to be protecting citizens. Moreover, he does not know who initially approved the machines—as in a panopticon, the center of control is invisible. Grover declares, "It's the most hideous creation ever conceived. No one can laugh, or joke. It *watches*, saps the very spirit. And the worse thing of all is I watch it. I can't not look. It's like a drug, a horrible drug. You can't resist it. It's an addiction."

In 1963, Grover's comment speaks to the addictive power of television as he describes its debilitating effect on the watchers as well as the watched. Throughout the episode, director Gerd Oswald and cinematographer Conrad Hall use low-key lighting and canted camera angles, and a monster-eye that recurs on the OBIT screen plays on the idea of television as a "one-eyed monster." In the final scene, the television screen literally becomes a monster. Dr. Scott, the Cypress Center's chairman, returns to testify. He had been hospitalized after suffering a breakdown because he could not stop spying on his wife, who was having an affair, though he could never see anyone with her on-screen. Scott solves the crime by deducing that Lomax, the one person who has never appeared on the OBIT screen, is both the interloper in his marriage and the murderer. Lomax then reveals himself as an alien whose species has created OBIT to prey on human weaknesses so that they will destroy themselves, making it easy to colonize the earth. The reveal was hinted at throughout the episode: scene by scene, the camera progressively closed in on Lomax, moving from medium shots to close-ups and finally to an extreme close-up of his heavy circular eyeglasses. Oswald explained, "I kept moving closer to him in stages, until I could focus on one of his eyes through his eyeglasses, and the reflections *in* the glass, to build the menace" (Schow 1998, 118).

The alien qua Lomax gives a final speech that summarizes the episode's dire warning:

> The machines are everywhere. Oh, you'll find them all-
> you're a zealous people. And you'll make a great show out

The camera gradually grows closer to Lomax (Jeff Corey) by focusing on his glasses in "OBIT."

of smashing a few of them, but for everyone you destroy, hundreds of others will be built, and they'll demoralize you, break your spirit, create such rifts and tensions in your society no one will be able to repair them. You're a savage, despairing planet. And when we come here to live, your friendless, demoralized flotsam will fall without a shot being fired. . . . You're all of the same dark persuasion. You demand, insist on knowing every private thought and hunger in everyone. Your families, your neighbors, everyone but yourselves.

The overriding message of "OBIT" is that surveillance—whether by government or individuals who watch one another—debilitates rather than defends society. At a time before home computers or

Lomax (Jeff Corey) reveals himself as an alien being at the end of "OBIT."

social media, "OBIT" sounds an alarm about social control, the loss of privacy in exchange for entertainment, and the potential for media to demoralize and divide, showing the pervasiveness and dangers of the prurient need to know the details of others' lives. Just as Colonel Grover despairs and says, "I can't not watch," Dr. Scott demonstrates how watching becomes an obsession that destroys people's lives. As Lomax's speech makes clear, the end result tears at the social fabric. Sconce summarizes, "Exploiting the insatiable American desire to know the secrets of both outer space and the family next door, the aliens are confident that this nation of atomized, isolated, and alienated citizens can be brought to its knees. A fragmented and distrustful society connected only through the dull glow of television screens is no match for this seductive technology of surveillance, one that allows these estranged citizens to spy on one another's personal traumas and family secrets" (1997, 32).

While the circular OBIT machine looks like an early television set, the observers who stare at its screen in darkened rooms throughout the episode make it seem even more like a home computer. As is the case today with social media, people spend their time staring at screens, observing the behaviors and actions of others. As Lomax asserts, it is not difficult to create rifts and tensions in human society—just give people the means and they will do it themselves.

After Lomax disappears, the final shot is a "high-angle, omniscient-god point of view . . . as though everyone is still being quietly watched" (Schow 1998, 118). The episode's lack of clear resolution intensifies its critique of surveillance: Lomax is exposed, and the machines will be destroyed, but the threat they pose is not contained. The Control Voice warns viewers and implores them to act: "In the last analysis dear friends, whether OBIT lives up to its name or not, depends entirely on you." Throughout the episode, the "Peeping Tom" nature of OBIT has implicated the viewer: we watch them watch as we are watched. The self-reflexive critique of technology and its maladaptive uses presented in the guise of science fiction tech noir heightens rather than allays anxieties.

"The Architects of Fear"

"The Architects of Fear" was the first episode fully produced by Stefano and aired as the third episode of the series. While less overtly reflexive than "The Galaxy Being" or "OBIT," "The Architects of Fear" uses fear of nuclear holocaust as a frame within which to warn of the dangers of technology, represented by overreaching science and the instrumentalist rationality that guides it. It is an episode *about* fear that exploits real terrors: of nuclear holocaust, the powers and perils of science, the secrecy and deception of experts entrusted with protecting the citizenry, and dehumanization as a consequence of technocratic society. It focuses on the question of identity, on what it means to be human, through a metamorphosis plot based on a genetically modified human—a posthuman prototype—created to prevent warring factions of the earth from destroying one another. When the episode first aired, several ABC affiliates blacked out the screen or showed the episode after the 11 p.m. news because they deemed the human-alien hybrid to be "disturbing to young minds" (Schow 1998, 70). The monster, designed by Projects Unlimited and played by a stuntman and acrobat, Janos Prohaska, was technically quite difficult to create. According to Schow, "The enormous headpiece sculpted by Wah Chang included functional eyelids, pulsating veins, and a bellows mouth all operated by a network of air cylinders. Pulaska was sealed into a rubberroid skin, canted plungingly forward on his stilts, his vision limited to what he could see out of the Thetan's 'nose' while wearing a head four times the size of his own" (1998, 67).

The opening images of the episode are as anxiety-provoking as the monster: what appears to be news footage of a flying object streaking across the sky, followed by panicked crowds fleeing. The object seen closer up is a nuclear missile, and the crowd becomes more chaotic as the sound of the approaching missile is amplified. A narrator's voice

The alien-human hybrid in "Architects of Fear."

intones, "Is this the day? Is this the beginning of the end? There is no time to wonder. No time to ask why is it happening, why is it finally happening. There is time only for fear, for the piercing pain of panic. Do we pray? Or do we merely run now and pray later? Will there be a later? Or is this the day?" The statement is followed by the image of an atomic bomb detonating amid the sounds of an explosion. The camera pulls back to reveal that the images are from a newsreel being watched by a group of scientists assembled in a darkened conference room. As is characteristic of *The Outer Limits*, the episode is noir science fiction that merges science fiction with expressionist techniques. The opening is shot in near-blackness, which creates an atmosphere of menace. Expository dialogue reveals that the men have formed a secret society at a place called United Labs. While their intentions appear benevolent—they are dedicated to the preservation

71

of world peace—they plan to do so by manipulating global politics and altering the genetic code of a human being, essentially dehumanizing one of their own. In an eerie scene, again shot in near-blackness, the group's leader, Dr. Gainer, refers to the opening images of potential nuclear holocaust as the fourth "near miss" and presents the reasoning behind the plan: "I don't care what reading of history you take, the pattern's the same. When a bacteria invasion strikes, when a fire rages, or a mad beast roams the streets, then and only then do men stop fighting each other and work to save themselves. A common fear, a common enemy, that is the only answer. If all the men of earth are threatened by an alien invasion from another planet."

In an attempt to prevent nuclear disaster, the scientists scheme to simulate an alien invasion so that the nations of the earth will align against a more fearful foe. Their plan is a basic propaganda tool—the externalization of fears onto an other as a tool of unification. In order to execute their plan, they will create a "scarecrow": a human transformed into an alien whom they will propel into space. Upon reentry, the alien will land at the United Nations General Assembly and warn that others will follow unless the people of Earth learn to coexist peacefully. The plan mimics the plot of *The Day the Earth Stood Still* (1951), where the alien Klaatu similarly addresses the United Nations and warns humanity that if they do not learn to live in harmony, they will be destroyed. But here the invasion is simulated. The scientists draw lots to determine who will be the test case, and the task falls to a physicist, Allen Leighton (Robert Culp).

After Allen agrees to the experiment, they inject him with the genetic material of a Thetan creature they claim to have captured.

Throughout, the episode contrasts the familiar domestic world of the known with the technocratic unknown. Stefano adds a melodramatic subplot to writer Meyer Dolinsky's story, a structural technique common in science fiction stories that aired as part of prestigious dramatic anthologies and one that facilitates identification with characters. The subplot involves Allen and his wife Yvette's (Geraldine Brooks)

Lighting and composition create an atmosphere of menace in "Architects of Fear."

struggle to have a child, visually conveyed through the recurrent motif of a store called From Here to Maternity. According to Schow, "Stefano wanted strongly to make shows that looked like feature films instead of run-of-the-mill TV, and with 'Architects,' both he and *The Outer Limits* hit their stride" (1998, 64). Throughout, Allen and Yvette are shot in a pattern of medium shots and close-ups accompanied by lush music, in contrast to the cold, impersonal domain of science as conveyed through chiaroscuro lighting and off-kilter framing. The lab is dark and imposing, filled with the complex machinery of science: X-ray devices, computers, fluoroscopes, surgical tables, tubes, and whirring gadgetry. Once Allen undergoes his transformation, he is shown only in silhouette, obscured behind a screen that conceals his body. The horror is hidden from viewers in order to heighten tension.

"The Architects of Fear" appears in a social and political milieu characterized by both fear of technology and faith in its possibilities. 73

But rather than affirming that people should put unbridled faith in science and the bureaucratic institutions that are supposed to be dedicated to their protection, the episode warns that science and technology devoid of human values is at best ineffective, and at worst immoral and duplicitous. The scientists fake Allen's death in order to work unimpeded, though Yvette senses that he is still alive. She attempts to enter the lab, but Dr. Gainer physically bars her from gaining entry, underscoring that she belongs in the domestic sphere. Both viewers—and Allen who is hidden from her—learn that she has conceived when Dr. Gainer orders her, "Go home. You have a baby to think about now."

The scientists' shortsighted reasoning is contrasted with Yvette's intuition and common sense; similarly, the male repression of emotion contrasts with her access to her feelings. Most important, Yvette's emotions do not conflict with her ability to reason; in fact, she is more rational than the scientific experts. Before Allen begins his transformation, he explains his decision to Yvette by reiterating the argument that a "scarecrow" will unite people through fear. Yvette's retort pulls the curtain back from the "experts," who have never ascertained exactly how they will accomplish their goal: "Most scarecrows don't even scare crows."

After Allen learns that Yvette is pregnant, he attempts to reclaim his humanity before it is too late. In an explosive scene, he smashes lab equipment and attacks the scientists who confine him. He expresses his resentment as he terrorizes his cohorts, turning against the creators who asked him to make this inhumane sacrifice. He tries to phone Yvette, but the scientists cut him off before he reaches her. Similar to "The Galaxy Being," he goes on a rampage prior to the narrative's attempt to restore order. He is on the cusp between who he was and what he will become.

There is one final moment of hesitation. When Allen is stabilized after his breakdown, he expresses his fear that the mission will fail. Dr. Gainer reassures him with a military metaphor: "Millions of soldiers have gone into war with less odds and less cause." Allen answers, "Thanks, I needed that." As Meeler and Hill write, the posthuman in film is often an intentional creation of governments seeking to create and control a "perfect soldier" (2015, 280). As such, Allen again represses his feelings and accepts the necessity of his sacrifice. Sontag writes that science fiction films of the 1950s were often ambivalent about dehumanization, presenting it as both a horror and an expression of the utopian fantasy of a unified world guided by reason. She describes films such as *The Invasion of the Body Snatchers* (1956), where humans are taken over by aliens, and observes, "Once the deed has been done, the victim is eminently satisfied with his condition;" further, she suggests that the victim has become "the very model of technocratic man, purged of emotions, volition-less, tranquil, obedient to all orders" (1965, 47). Allen becomes acquiescent to the "architects of fear" and accepts their logic. But unlike science fiction films that "offer a new version of the oldest romance of all-of the strong invulnerable hero with the mysterious lineage come to do battle on behalf of good and against evil" (44), Allen is a tragic figure who represents the dangers of misguided science and the folly of those who blindly follow.

Allen/the alien is launched into space, but the navigation system goes awry almost immediately. Allen, now a hideous creature, crashes near the laboratory. The plan never came close to being executed, an indication of how poorly conceived it was from the start. According to Rapchak, the ending is "the cruelest sort of irony, a bitter, devastating denouement in the manner of the classic, fatalistic tragedies" (2011). In the closing scene, suspense is maintained by casting the grotesque body in shadows and hiding it behind shrubbery. Allen encounters a group of duck hunters whose dog barks in fear, after which the body is seen in entirety for the first time. The terrified hunters fire on him—a comment on the human propensity for violence.

At the lab, Yvette recoils at the wounded, monstrous body, but as Wildermuth observes, "she is taken aback but does not react in

Yvette (Geraldine Brooks) is center frame as she condemns the "Architects of Fear."

uncontrolled fear; she is center screen in the slightly low-angle close-up that underscores her self-control and agency here" (2014, 73). As the alien is dying, she recognizes that he is/was Allen by their secret sign; he makes a hand gesture that promises to protect her from evil. She embraces the monster, then faces his cohorts and accuses them of signing his death warrant: "Men like you using tricks. A scarecrow will change everything. You killed him and *for what?*"

"The Architects of Fear" has been referred to as *Dr. Jekyll and Mr. Hyde* for the Atomic Age (Samerdyke 2017), though in this case a man becomes a monster to try to save rather than destroy the world. Most crucially, it ponders the nature of identity. At what point is Allen no longer human? At what point do the humans become monstrous? Allen is genetically modified to become an alien, so that he no longer has the physical attributes of a human. He has become "other," so that his death is the only possible way to restore "normality." While many science fiction films in the 1950s used aliens as metaphors for Communism, aliens were, as Hill points out, "simply a version of the broader tendency of 'othering,' of projecting the negative, repressed aspects of the self, either individually or collectively, onto other people or cultures, thereby demonizing them" (2008, 117). In "The Architects of Fear," the scientists attempt to create the alien other as a "scarecrow" for people to project their fears onto, but it is a projection of their own fear. Instead of the alien, the scientists are the true "monstrous" other; in the guise of rationality, they represent irrationality and the impulse to resort to aggression before reason that is the worst of human nature. The real threat comes from overzealous scientific experimentation guided solely by instrumentalist aims.

But, in contrast to conventional science fiction where a male protagonist defeats the threat, the episode turns Yvette into the protagonist. Her ability to combine reason with intuition and compassion serves as a condemnation of the masculinist "architects of fear." Wildermuth observes, "Yvette's indictment is deeply impassioned at the end but also crystal clear in its rational assessment of the crime these men committed against humanity. She can at least win a moral victory and make possible a moral lesson—even though her wisdom comes at a terrible price" (2014, 74).

"The Architects of Fear" shows us the horror of technology. It asks us to consider the morality of men who would turn one of their own into a monster and shows us the hubris of science and technology, where expertise comes at the expense of wisdom. It demonstrates the futility of achieving peace through a weapon of war. Rypel sums up the episode's conclusion: "In one of TOL's most harrowing glimpses of human technological effort, even science fiction's most noble stereotypes—philanthropic scientists—endeavor to achieve their lofty inspiration by laying a foundation of deceit. And their complex fabrication of fear ironically destroys two people who share a simple and beautiful love and understanding which might be the real answer to peaceful co-existence" (1977, 20). The episode ends on a typically bleak note, and the Control Voice's final summation serves as both a warning and advice:

> Scarecrows and magic and other fatal flaws do not bring people closer together. There is no magic substitute for soft caring and hard work, for self-respect and mutual love. If we can learn from the mistake these frightened men made, then their mistake will not only have been grotesque; it will have been at least a lesson, a lesson at last to be learned.

4

THE OUTER LIMITS AS CREATIVE ADAPTATION

Chapter 4 considers the influence of antecedent texts on *The Outer Limits*. I assess how the series' writers and producers engage in creative borrowing by adapting all or parts of material from other sources. *The Outer Limits'* first season consisted of thirty-two episodes; the rapid production schedule led to the recycling of material, either literally by incorporating material from films or other television shows, or by reworking images and ideas drawn from print or visual media. Moreover, as an anthology series whose episodes did not adhere to a rigid format, *The Outer Limits* came together as a bricolage of different genres, themes, and tropes. Stefano lauded the show's "fragmentation," which he believed wouldn't have been possible in a series with continuing characters. In his words, "The entire body of work of *The Outer Limits* is like a gigantic, mirrored ceiling that is broken, and the moment you tried to get one character to tie all of those pieces together, you'd have nothing" (Rypel 1977, 55).

Contemporary adaptation studies assume that most texts are derivative, but what is important is how they combine different elements to "create an aggregate effect, a new flavor . . . that recalls yet escapes from that elemental past" (Telotte 2012, xxii). Throughout season 1, *The Outer Limits*' multilayered adaptations conveyed a consistent vision, in Stefano's words, of "Science Fiction in relation to, or against, or to the improvement or detriment of the race that inhabits our own earth" (Schow 1998, 354). As he stated in "The Canons," "Out of the issues and human conditions of this our time, out of the north- and south-seeking poles of human impulses and behaviors, out of the world AS WE KNOW IT come the themes which are the warp and woof of our dramas" (353). Writers were asked to dramatize contemporary issues—preferably those that they felt strongly about—through the lens of science fiction. In this way, while *The Outer Limits* often borrowed material from the past, it recombined images and ideas in order to comment on the present and, perhaps, to speculate on the future. The way the series wove together images and ideas in what Stefano described as "the imaginative and inventive loom of Science Fiction" (353) transformed them into something new and made *The Outer Limits* more than a mere pastiche of earlier forms.

Authorship and Adaptation

The question of authorship haunts adaptation studies, especially in a genre like science fiction, where writers frequently borrow from their predecessors. While *The Outer Limits* relied heavily on adaptation, in at least two cases later works of science fiction would be accused of taking its ideas. The most famous case involved writer Harlan Ellison, who wrote two episodes of *The Outer Limits* during its second season. Ellison adapted "Soldier" (1964), his first science fiction television script, from his own short story, "Soldier of Tomorrow," published in *Fantastic Universe Science Fiction* in 1957. He also wrote an original script for the series, "Demon with a Glass Hand," which went on to win a Writer's Guild Award for Outstanding Television Anthology Script in the 1964–65 season.

Both "Soldier" and "Demon with a Glass Hand" deal with cyborgs and time travel from the future to the past, though "Soldier" is the episode that Ellison would claim had been plagiarized in James

Cameron's 1984 film *Terminator*. The 1985 review of *Terminator* in *Cinefantastique* refers to it as both "derivative and original at the same time," a claim that can equally be applied to any number of episodes of *The Outer Limits* and science fiction films. As Brennan points out, the first three minutes of *Terminator* and "Soldier" are visually similar, from the depiction of a postapocalyptic landscape, to visual imagery of the time travel effect, to the fact that both time travelers arrive in an alley. But *Terminator* begs the question of when a media text is paying homage to its predecessors in order to reinvigorate ideas—for example, in "Soldier," which aired in the midst of the Cold War, the threat to humankind is represented by aliens, whereas twenty years later the threat is presented as an artificial intelligence network. Is this an adaptation or an original idea? Science fiction has a history of reworking themes through creative borrowing, drawing deep from the well of myth, literature, films, or other television programs. Considered from this angle, Cameron did not "steal" ideas any more than Stefano, who freely borrowed from classic literature when he declared that he was "giving a text a haircut." Both "Soldier" and *Terminator* were arguably based on the myth of Gilgamesh, which is cited in both the introduction and prologue of "Soldier," and pre-dated both "Soldier" and "Demon with a Glass Hand" by several hundred years. Cameron acknowledged his stylistic debt to *The Outer Limits* in an interview where he asserted, "If I really think the about the influences that helped shape the story, the entire feeling can be traced back to some '50s science fiction films and *Outer Limits* episodes. The thing that *The Outer Limits* had, that always impressed me visually, was its use of the deep focus film noir look of the '40s films and the German Expressionist movies of the '30s" (French 1996, 15). But Ellison was purportedly told by a friend that Cameron, when asked where he had gotten the idea for *The Terminator*, had replied, "I ripped off a couple of Harlan Ellison stories" (Brennan). But, as Hutcheon has written, "there are precious few stories around that have not been ripped off from somewhere" (quoted in Jowett and Abbott 2013, 57).

Nevertheless, Ellison contacted the film's financer, Hemdale Productions, and its distributor, Orion Pictures, and threatened legal action for plagiarism. Although Cameron disputed the charges, Hemdale and Orion settled for an undisclosed sum and an agreement that Ellison would be acknowledged on all future copies of the film.

In the case of the comic book series *Watchmen* (1986–87), writer Alan Moore was accused of stealing the idea for the ending of the series from *The Outer Limits* episode "The Architects of Fear." In both cases, the plot involves a faked alien invasion as a means of securing world peace. Purportedly, the book series editor, Len Wein, noted the similarity and asked Moore to change the ending to be more original. Moore refused, though he did belatedly acknowledge the similarities and referenced "The Architects of Fear" in the final comic. He explained, "Around issue 10, I came across a guide to cult television. There was an *Outer Limits* episode called 'The Architects of Fear.' I thought: 'Wow. That's a bit close to our story. In the last issue, we have a TV promoting that *Outer Limits* episode—a belated nod'" (Willaert 2015). Wein took the remediation even further, and in his prequel *Before Watchmen: Ozymandius* (2012), he gave even more credit to the series. In Wein's telling, the villain studies "The Architects of Fear" to see why the plan failed so that he can successfully carry out the invasion. The homage to "The Architects of Fear" continued in the 2009 film *Watchmen*, which closes with a scene from the television program. But even here, the origin of an idea is murky. As I mentioned in chapter 3, "The Architects of Fear" bore similarities to *The Day the Earth Stood Still*. Even more pertinent was a science fiction story "Invasion from Outer Space," written by Stan Lee and Larry Lieber and published in the 1959 issue of *Tales of Suspense*. The plot is virtually identical to that of "The Architects of Fear" and possibly inspired writer Meyer Dolinksy. But it is important to note that while all of these stories share a plot point, they are not mere replicas of one another. It is through the bricolage, through the piecing together of different ideas, styles, and genres, that something new emerges.

The Outer Limits as Adaptation

Adaptation was a common practice in both dramatic anthologies, where teleplays were often based on literary or theatrical works, and in science fiction and horror-based television anthologies, where stories were frequently taken from books or pulp magazines. Producer George Foley, for example, bought rights to more than two thousand science fiction stories for *Tales of Tomorrow*, while the majority of the episodes of the horror anthology *Thriller* were adapted from the magazine *Weird Tales*. *The Outer Limits*, which shared with *Thriller* many of the same writers, directors, and actors, similarly relied on material drawn from science fiction and horror. For example, "The Invisibles," written and produced by Stefano, was similar to Robert Heinlein's book *The Puppet Masters* (1951), serialized in *Galaxy Science Fiction*. *The Puppet Masters* uses alien invasion as a metaphor for Communism: aliens take the form of parasites who attach themselves to people's nervous systems and control their minds. A secret branch of the CIA investigates, and though the aliens manage to infiltrate even the military sent to fight them, in the end the government agents find a way to destroy them and restore order. In contrast, "The Invisibles" critiques the way corruption "infects" powerful institutions. Here a secret government organization, called the GIA, is the source rather than the remedy for the problem. As Schow states, "It renders the military-industrial complex as literally diseased, infected by a cancer cell-like extraterrestrial, but presses home the point that such a plague would not thrive without the vanity and greed of 'men in places so high, no one knows how high they are,' as General Clarke says in the episode" (1998, 169). Without specifically referring to "The Invisibles," Stefano made his intentions clear in a 2000 *LA Times* interview, where he was asked whether the guise of science fiction allowed him to address controversial themes:

Oh absolutely. It absolutely served that purpose. I was writing things that were anti-CIA. If I had gone to any network and said I had an idea for a show that was anti-CIA, they would have thrown me out. Here we had monsters and aliens that took the curse off it. We had just come out of a strange dark period. The '50s as we look back on them now, we know the harm that was done and then a few of us sensed that something was wrong and we got to write shows about it. (King 2000)

"The Invisibles" is noir science fiction that creates a tense, ominous mood throughout. Moreover, similar to Stefano's adaption of the film *The Purple Heart* in "Nightmare," the ending avoids *The Puppet Masters'* tidy resolution. As in "Nightmare" and most other episodes of *The Outer Limits*, "The Invisibles" leaves viewers feeling anxious rather than reassured. The wounded soldier barely escapes from the parasitic alien; he (and the viewer) is left with the thought that the menace is everywhere. Stefano related, "We wanted to say things that had both a dramatic and intellectual impact, and we were looking to for ways to open people's minds to alien things—alien philosophies, creatures, cultures. Writers are essentially missionaries without portfolio, and the show gave us a way to say things that were very close to our hearts" (Schow 1998, 80).

In most cases, Stefano relied on a cadre of writers and directors, many of whom circulated among shows such as *Alfred Hitchcock Presents*, *The Twilight Zone*, and *Thriller*. As a result, influences and interrelations could get quite complex. For example, in 1964, Charles Beaumont, who wrote more than twenty episodes of *The Twilight Zone*, submitted a script to Stefano called "An Ordinary Town." It was similar to "Valley of the Shadow," a *Twilight Zone* episode he had written the year before. In both episodes, a bucolic small town is not what it seems. In "Valley of the Shadow," when a visitor arrives, the townspeople use 84 alien technology to imprison him within an invisible shield, with the promise that he will never age, but he can never leave. In "An Ordinary Town," the townspeople only exist as the projection of a giant alien brain, so that there is no way out for the errant protagonist.

But Stefano chose not to produce "An Ordinary Town" as written. According to Schow, he was looking for material "with a heavier than usual emphasis on the Gothic" (1998, 212). He turned to writer Donald S. Sanford to revise the script. Sanford had written fifteen episodes of *Thriller*, including the Gothic horror story "The Incredible Doktor Markesan," itself based on a story published in *Weird Tales*. Sanford's revision became "The Guests." He kept the concept of an alien brain that projects illusory images, though in keeping with the Gothic sensibility of "The Incredible Doktor Markesan," it creates the illusion of an isolated Victorian mansion rather than the small town portrayed in Beaumont's original script. In all three versions, a nefarious creature, whether an alien or, in Doktor Markesan's case, a zombie, attempts to confine the protagonist, though they offer him eternal life in exchange. Otherwise, Sanford's revision departs from Beaumont's script. In his version, a young drifter, Wade (Geoffrey Horne), stops his car when he sees an elderly man dying on the side of the road. Seeking help, he happens upon a mansion, which is occupied by three elderly, mean-spirited residents and a fourth, a beautiful young woman.

As Stefano requested, the episode had a bleak tone that recalled Sanford's work on "The Incredible Doktor Markesan." Both episodes take place in a decrepit mansion with a baroque set design. Shuttered windows, cobwebbed ceilings, dark hallways, and winding staircases are augmented by chiaroscuro lighting, eerie music, unsettling sound effects, and canted camera angles. As is typical of Gothic fiction, the decaying mansion symbolizes the inner state of the characters who reside within it. According to Muir, the house in Gothic fiction "appears to be haunted both by an external, self-organizing supernatural force and by the personal, individual secrets and sins of the human dwellers within" (2004). However, while Doktor Markesan sells his soul for eternal life, in "The Guests" the inhabitants of the mansion embody "sins" of greed, cruelty, and vanity. Moreover, Sanford uses the episode to relate the past to the present: Wade's leather jacket, jeans, sunglasses, and convertible jalopy code him as a beatnik, in contrast to the residents of the house who dress and behave anachronistically. Wade learns that, beginning in 1928, they have been imprisoned by an alien "brain" that dissects their thoughts in order to quantify and thus comprehend the human race. But it becomes apparent that the alien's "prisoners" choose to live in the past rather than leave, which is given added resonance due to the casting of aging actress Gloria Grahame, who essentially plays herself as a faded film star. Her portrayal of a vain, once-famous actress living in the past is another creative adaptation that recalls both Norma Desmond in the classic Gothic noir *Sunset Boulevard* (1950) and *The Twilight Zone*'s "16-Millimeter Shrine" (1959).

The result is more than simply Gothic science fiction. As Muir points out, the Gothic compositions rooted in the past are disrupted by the forward-looking avant-garde imagery of Surrealism (2014). As a result, the episode's "borrowings" are pitted against one another through the frame of science fiction. For example, when Wade first realizes that he is imprisoned in the house, the alien, who controls the residents from the upper level, pulls him upstairs and leads him through a labyrinth of corridors. All is black; Wade sees only abstract, Escher-like images of floating Greek columns, geometric shapes, and doors that open into emptiness.

These dream-like images, linked to no clear referent, mark the intrusion of the fantastic and, as in surrealism, "create an imaginary realm suspended between the conscious and the unconscious, between the mundane and the extraordinary" (Berger 2014, 21). Not coincidentally, Wade's first question upon entering the house is "Is this a dream?," and references to dreams and illusions recur throughout the episode. Muir describes Wade's journey:

Wade (Geoffrey Horne) encounters geometric shapes and doors that lead nowhere in "The Guests."

> The cardinal struggle takes place not just within the four (windowless) walls of the looming and convenient mansion at its center, but also—or perhaps primarily—deep within Wade Norton's consciousness. The irrational, ethereal events that occur there comprise a test that will lead him, ultimately, to the responsibility and reason of adulthood, or the stagnant hell of a lifetime of puerile self-deception. (2014)

Berger's comments on surrealism in *The Twilight Zone* equally apply to "The Guests": "Trapped in a multitude of existential nightmares, its characters lived in a perpetual crisis of identity, fueled by a world that was often at the precipice of extinction. Such fantasies were never far from the minds of viewers, caught up in Cold War hysteria and gripped by the fear of nuclear annihilation" (2014, 22).

The alien, a gelatinous brain-like blob, is a scientist of sorts who is trying to produce an algorithm that will define humanity and predict its fate, another example of *The Outer Limits'* critique of overzealous science. He shows Wade his equation; a screen behind him projects images (taken from stock footage) that he has pulled out of the minds of those in the house—a family, work, faith, and art—which the alien defines as positives, though these are countered by negatives—images of destruction, fear, hopelessness, and, finally hate, the latter visualized by an atomic bomb explosion. It is the negative images, the alien claims, that will assure the destruction of the human race, though he is puzzled because he knows that part of the equation is still missing. Like all rational systems, the alien technology can extract information, but it cannot access emotions. His inability to complete the equation shows the limits of a science devoid of values.

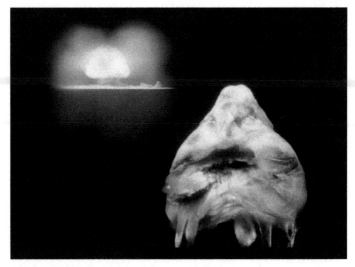

The alien shows Wade images that will assure the destruction of the human race.

The episode takes on another layer and builds the plot through yet another adaptation. Like "The Bellero Shield," discussed in chapter 2 as a retelling of *Macbeth*, "The Man Who was Never Born," which places the mythic "Beauty and the Beast" within a futuristic science fiction frame, and "The Sixth Finger," inspired by George Bernard Shaw's *Back to Methuselah* (1921), "The Guests" draws from literature, in this case Nathaniel Hawthorne's short story "Rappicini's Daughter," published in 1884 (also adapted in a televised episode of *Lights Out*). "Rappicini's Daughter," an early example of Gothic science fiction, is both an admonitory tale about the perils of science and an account of a doomed romance. In the story, a medical researcher in medieval Padua teaches his daughter Beatrice to care for his poisonous plants. She becomes immune to the poison, but is confined to the garden because she poses a danger to others. A young man meets her in the garden and falls in love with her, but then he becomes poisonous too. The story warns of blind devotion to science that ignores the human cost, turning an innocent girl into a monster. In "The Guests," the alien attempting to "scientifically" study the human race replaces the father. The episode invokes "Rappicini's Daughter" when Wade falls in love with Tess, the young woman who stayed in the house to be with her father, who initially hid in the house to avoid being charged with fraud. It was his body that Wade had found by the side of the road (though the father's departure is not explained). But, like Beatrice, Tess is complicit with the "sin" of her father, and she too has turned monstrous because she does not age. In Hawthorne's story, Beatrice's lover attempts to save her by providing her (and himself) with an antidote, though it kills her while he survives. "The Guests" takes a different turn: Wade does not try to bring Tess into the outside world, but instead offers to live with her forever inside the illusion constructed by the alien. In order to free him, Tess walks through the gate and immediately begins to age. Her body crumbles to dust as Wade stares in horror (the sudden aging of an eternally beautiful woman is also reminiscent of H. Rider Haggard's 1886 novel *She*). But unlike "Rappicini's Daughter," and unlike most episodes of *The Outer Limits*, despite Tess's death "The Guests" ends on a (somewhat) positive note. The alien realizes that the human capacity for love, which can't be quantified, is the missing part of the equation. He orders Wade to "Go out of this dream," after which, the experiment complete, the alien transforms the house back into a giant brain and then dissolves into nothingness.

The horror of seeing the heroine of the story transformed into dust, as well as the mansion that takes the form of a giant brain before disappearing entirely, is somewhat mitigated by the ending, when the alien frees Wade to rejoin the world. He has avoided living in a past that is safe but stagnant, and he moves into a future open to possibilities. In the end, the episode answers the question of what makes us human with a message that presages the hippie movement that would come to define the 1960s. Love is the unquantifiable element that defines humanity; as the alien tells Wade, he has learned that love can conquer hate and fear, and so humans might not destroy themselves after all. As Muir concludes, "That is the illusion we must battle, argues 'The Guests.' We can choose love over hate, individuality over conformity, and escape over imprisonment. We can solve the human equation *to our liking*, and not to the tune of tradition or convention" (2014). By taking a science fiction story and combining it with both Gothic tropes and a literary classic, "The Guests" explores reality and illusion, past and present, the rationality of science and the unquantifiable nature of emotion.

Creative Adaptation and the Art Film

Perhaps more so than literature or television, cinema exerted an important influence on *The Outer Limits*. As Baxter observes, one of the main reasons for the series' success was "the overall control of Joseph Stefano, whose knowledge of and interest in the cinema show through continually" (1970, 193). Lucas notes, "*The Outer Limits* was meant to be art rather than conventional television. Not only was it shot on 35 mm film, but visuals were calibrated for how they would look on dailies, not on TV" (2018). The episode "The Forms of Things Unknown" showed the influence of European art films, which made it even more of an anomaly on network television. European art films, typified by Italian neorealism, the symbolic imagery of Ingmar Bergman, and the French New Wave, became popular in the post–World War II period as taste cultures, rather than economic status, emerged as ways to differentiate mainstream and elite audiences (Krasinewski, 84). According to Gomery, "Generally, audience studies found that art theatres attracted persons of above-average education, more men than women, and many solitary moviegoers. This was the crowd that attended the opera, theatre, lectures, and ballet" (1992, 189). It was not typically the audience for lowbrow science fiction television programs.

Initially, Stevens aligned himself with the art film when he moved to Hollywood and established Daystar. His first feature film, *Private Property* (1960), was described as "[living] somewhere between the bleak, erotically charged film noir . . . and later art house thrillers about postwar excess" (Deighan 2016). *Variety* wrote that the industry "was watching the film as a possible forerunner of an American 'new wave' movement" ("Is There an American" 1960, 4), while *Time* announced in its review that "Director Stevens and Producer Colbert have carried the New Wave into the heart of Hollywood" ("New Wavelet" 1960, 69). But the film received limited distribution in the United States because its "adult" themes, while typical of foreign films, failed to meet the Hayes Production Code. Stevens's two later films were less ambitious, though he returned to form when he became producer of *The Outer Limits*.

Stefano was also a devotee of the art film whose screenwriting career became established when Alfred Hitchcock hired him to adapt Robert Bloch's novel *Psycho* (1960) for the screen. As noted on the blog Creative Screenwriting, Hitchcock wanted to make a popular low-budget film that was at the same time "a more intelligent and astonishing film in the vein of Henri-Georges Clouzot's *Les Diaboliques* (1955)" (2018). According to Castle, the horror boom in the late 1950s and early 1960s was initiated by the success of *Les Diaboliques*, a French film adapted from a best-selling book that introduced the psychological thriller to European and American audiences (Jancovich 2018, 31). *Psycho*, following *Les Diaboliques*, merged the tropes of the horror film with an art film aesthetic by making it a noir-like psychological study of madness that relied on the thriller's twists and turns.

When Stefano began producing *The Outer Limits*, he stated his desire to bring the art film to television. Gerani quotes him as saying, "In my first meeting with Connie [Conrad] Hall and John Nickolaus, I stated that I wanted these episodes to have the look of foreign films . . . foreign films at the time had a very special quality about them. Whether they were Bergmanesque or Japanese in feeling, there was something we were not doing over here, and *certainly* not in television" (1977, 56). "The Forms of Things Unknown" is Stefano's "Bergmanesque" adaption of *Les Diaboliques* that also references Shakespeare's *A Midsummer's Night's Dream* in the context of science fiction. In *Les Diaboliques*, the headmaster of a school, Michel, is murdered by his wife, Christina, who is in cahoots with his mistress, Nicole. They drown him in a bathtub and drop his body in the school's swimming pool, though his body does not surface when the pool is drained. Christina fears that Michel is still alive; at night, she senses that he is following her and runs to her room. In a surprise twist that likely influenced the famous shower scene in *Psycho*, Michel's body, submerged in the bathtub, rises out of the water. Christina has a heart attack and dies, though the end reveals that Nicole and Michel have arranged the fake murder.

In "The Forms of Things Unknown," which Stefano made with director Gerd Oswald, cinematographer Conrad Hall, and composer Dominic Frontiere, Stefano draws from *Les Diaboliques* and the imagery of art films, even setting the episode in France rather than the United States. Beam notes that the episode is packed with "startling, compelling imagery that was generally exclusive to foreign films at the time" (2014). According to Gerani, "In a nutshell, it's 1964 prime-time television meets French New Wave, with enough German expressionism in the Old Dark House scenes to justify a 'scary show' classification" (2011). It was unlike any other episode of American television at the time—so much so that Schow observes, "It doesn't run against the grain of normal TV fare so much as attack it outright" (1998, 228).

The episode has no Control Voice, nor does it feature a BEAR. The opening scene in particular demonstrates both the influence of *Les Diaboliques* and the episode's unconventional style. After the teaser and opening credits, the episode begins with a disorienting shot of a speeding car, brakes screeching and horn honking, swerving precipitously down a winding country road; deliberately askew camera angles are intercut with close-ups of a grinning man at the wheel. A woman, initially hidden from view, sits beside him, coolly lighting a cigarette, and they begin kissing passionately as the car keels dangerously. There is a freeze frame, then, in contrast to the frenzied opening, the camera tracks across a still lake surrounded by trees, akin to the shot of a stagnant swimming pool that opens *Les Diaboliques*. The strums of a harp on the soundtrack and the deep-focus photography would suggest an idyllic scene, except for a disconcerting, high-pitched tone that accompanies the otherwise soothing sounds. The camera pans left to reveal what appears to be a naked man, Andre (Scott Marlowe), though branches in the foreground cover his lower extremities. The camera pans to reveal him wearing bathing trunks, though the scene remains erotically charged. There is a cut to the woman we saw in the car, Kassia (Vera Miles, who also appeared in *Psycho*), who stirs a drink. Andre enters the water and asks for his drink. Cut to a second woman, Leonora (Barbara Rush), who is picking leaves from a plant. The music becomes more ominous; there is an extreme close-up of Andre's lips, smiling smugly, then a cut to Kassia, who puts a leaf in a glass and shakes the concoction. Andre dominates the two women; when Kassia alone brings him the drink he also calls for Leonora and orders them, "Now both of you bring me my drink. Kassia will pour. Leonora will

Kassia (Vera Miles) and Leonora (Barbara Rush) wade into the water to serve Andre (Scott Marlowe) a fatal drink in "The Forms of Things Unknown."

serve. Come as you are . . . in your fine stiletto heels." Both women obediently wade into the water, fully clothed, in their high heeled shoes, and Kassia serves him the fatal concoction.

Like the two murderesses in *Les Diaboliques*, Kassia, dressed in white, is assertive and confident, while Leonora, in black, is more passive and fearful. In a visual flourish more typical of art films than network television, Andre's death scene is almost two minutes long, the camera alternating between extreme close-ups of Andre's lips as he laughs cruelly when the women enter the water to medium shots as they gradually approach him with the deadly drink. His body fills the frame as he falls into the water; the scene is almost abstract as the camera cuts to blurry trees overhead, reflections of sunlight, extreme close-ups of the water, Andre flailing, a swish pan from

Andre to Kassia and Leonora, a close-up of Andre holding out his hands, then a high-angle crane shot of the three figures standing in now-black water. Andre desperately tries to grab on to Kassia, who, in a close-up, gazes down impassively. His body goes under, then rises unexpectedly, until it finally submerges, with a final image of his silhouette seemingly shot from underwater. A wide-angle shot shows the two women leaving, though the camera focuses on Leonora, who nervously looks back at the body bobbling in the water.

To calm Leonora's fears, Kassia drags Andre's body into the trunk of the car and they drive on. In a dreamlike sequence that evokes a Bergman film, they encounter a funeral procession that culminates when one of the participants throws a rose at their windscreen. There is a sudden thunderstorm, and the latch to the trunk pops open. Like her counterpart in *Les Diaboliques*, Leonora fears that their victim is still alive. Kassia stops the car to show her that Andre is indeed dead, but Leonora thinks she sees him blink and flees into the woods. Kassia finds her and almost convinces her that Andre is dead. In a device characteristic of the classic horror films of Val Lewton, whom Stefano cited as an influence, Leonora sees Andre's silhouette appear in the rainy woods, though when Kassia turns nothing is there (Schow 1998, 234). Leonora returns to the car, though this time Andre's body is indeed gone. Now frantic, she runs back into the woods, with Kassia in pursuit. She arrives at a desolate mansion and bangs on the door. Colas, a blind man dressed in a butler's coat, opens the door and offers them shelter.

Here, at the end of the opening set-up, the plot departs from *Les Diaboliques*. The episode turns into science fiction, though the question of whether the victim is alive or dead that animates *Les Diaboliques* remains central. It becomes even more entrenched in what Gerani refers to as "Mr. Stefano's most liberating psycho-session on celluloid, his feelings, thoughts and impressions given free rein in an oblique 'story' that allows for unprecedented, over the top experimentation" (2011). Colas, who despite his attire is the owner of the house, is host to a young man, Tone Hobart, who has created a "time-tilting machine" that brings the dead back to life. Even the hallway leading to his workroom consists of odd angles and false perspectives, created by building the set with very high ceilings, walls that tilted inward the higher they rose, and lightbulbs strung across it (Lucas 2018). The hallway leads to Tone's time machine, in a tiny room full of ticking clocks and wires radiating in all directions that looks like an abstract work of modern art. Its disorienting effect is exaggerated when Leonora's image is inverted as she first enters.

Clocks become an aural and visual motif in the episode, through the sounds of ticking that emanate from Tone's machine and permeate the house, as well as through a broken clown clock on the mantelpiece. The clock represents Andre, who Tone repeatedly refers to as a

Leonora's image is inverted when she enters Tone's time machine in "The Forms of Things Unknown."

"clown" who, like the clock, can be brought back to life. A spinning toy ballerina holding a long pole to maintain balance is another recurring motif. The toy is often in the foreground while the characters are in soft focus in the background; most notably, its shadow dances on Leonora's face when she confesses her crime to Colas. Wissner argues that it functions, like a music box trope, as a signifier of nostalgia and a longing for simplicity and childhood. She also notes that Dominic Frontiere composed a waltz for the ballerina, though it is metrically off-center and unbalanced, which gives viewers a sense that something is wrong (2016, 151). The ballerina in balance, which represents an irretrievable past, serves as a counterpoint to the time-tilting machine that allows the past to become the present.

The episode's title, "The Forms of Things Unknown," is a line from Shakespeare's *A Midsummer's Night's Dream*, and like a Shakespearian play, its highly stylized language is poetic rather than expository. Tone even quotes a line from the play—"Such tricks have strong imagination"—when he refers to Leonora's belief that Andre is still alive, though he adds "that if it would only apprehend some joy." Both have a thematic relationship in that the central question revolves around reality and illusion, though in "The Forms of Things Unknown," Shakespeare's comedy of mistaken identity takes a tragic turn. Tone resurrects Andre, but then realizes he has made a mistake. In another example of the episode's stylized language, where characters perform philosophical soliloquys, Tone tells Colas that he should have seen that the time-tilting device was evil. Colas answers, "How could I have seen? I am blind." Tone responds, "The blind see those dark things. So many loved people have died, Colas. In my time and before my time. I worried about what would become of the love left over. So I built an antidote. And allowed it to resurrect an evil clown. I am not the man to tinker with time, Colas. That man is God." The episode ends in death: Andre leaves with Kassia, who becomes distraught after abandoning Leonora and jumps from the car. Andre tries to run her down, but he crashes the car and dies again. Tone, who originally brought himself back to life, asks Leonora to destroy the machine after he returns to the "safe, dead quiet of the past." Kassia returns in time to join Leonora, and Kassia, Colas, and Leonora watch Tone enter the machine and vanish. The Control Voice asks viewers to tune in next week, though this would be the last episode produced by Stevens and Stefano.

According to Stevens, "It was an extraordinary and peculiar piece. But not a coherent thing for an ordinary audience to grab. It was perceived as being far too 'arty'" (Schow 1998, 235). Stefano himself admitted that his little "foreign film" clearly wasn't for all tastes, "challenging unsuspecting viewers with a double-barreled creative assault of both heavily stylized visuals and dialogue" (Gerani, 2011). In this regard, the episode's Shakespearean title can be read as Stefano's self-reflection on the creative process that turns imagination into art:

> The poet's eye, in fine Frenzy rolling
> Doth glance from Heaven to Earth,
> For as earth to heaven
> And as Imagination bodies forth
> The forms of things unknown. The poet's pen
> Turns them to shapes and gives to any nothing
> A local habitation and a name.

Despite Stefano's attempt to bring art film sensibilities to television, when he submitted the script to ABC in December 1963, they rejected it as "too different, too strange" (Schow 1998, 228). Yet, oddly, they reversed their decision and asked him to create one version for *The Outer Limits* and to rewrite it without any science fiction elements as the pilot for a Gothic horror program called *The Unknown*. Stefano rewrote the script in eleven days, this time with Kassia and Andre faking his death, and with Tone as a madman rather than a time traveler.

Stefano, encouraged by Stevens, saw *The Unknown* as his opportunity to direct, produce, and write, much as Stevens had done for both *Stoney Burke* and *The Outer Limits*. But at a time when networks were expanding their control, ABC balked at the idea of a "triple-hyphenate." Stevens and Dominic Frontiere protested to ABC on Stefano's behalf, and Stevens threatened not to deliver the next six *Outer Limits* episodes. As he proclaimed, "That's why networks don't like artists in control. A business manager never would have dreamed of opposing the establishment that way" (Schow 1998, 229). Although Stefano backed down, it was too late. Stevens observed, "We had to be disciplined, cut down, and put back into our place" (235). Although *The Outer Limits*' ratings were decent, it was at this point that ABC decided to cut its budget and move it to Saturday nights for season 2. As mentioned in the introduction, both Stevens and Stefano saw this as an attempt to end the show. Though both retained ownership and remained on the credits as producers, they made no contributions to season 2. But by combatting ABC, Stevens effectively insured the demise of Daystar. According to Stevens, "The artist sometimes puts art above anything. And when he does that, he's not in the industry anymore" (237).

None of Stevens's proposed television pilots were picked up, and though he secured enough funding to make *Incubus* (1966), a horror/film noir starring William Shatner that was written entirely in Esperanto, it was Daystar's final feature film, and the company went out of business soon afterward. ABC also decided not to option Stefano's pilot for *The Unknown*. Both Stevens and Stefano continued to write for television, and both became consulting advisors on the reboot of *The Outer Limits* (1995–2002). But their "great adventure" came to an end, and the abbreviated season 2 was more conventional.

5

BEYOND *THE OUTER LIMITS*

Just as *The Outer Limits'* mix of horror and science fiction drew on antecedent texts, its reach extended to television programs that followed. Chapter 5 tracks its influence on *Star Trek* (1966–69), which employed many of the same creative personnel as *The Outer Limits* and similarly used science fiction to indirectly address contemporary issues. Both shows attracted cult followings after they went off the air. With the rise of cable in the late 1980s, channels that aimed to reach niche audiences took advantage of the strong fandom associated with science fiction series and led to a host of new programs in the 1990s. Booker gives much of the credit for the genre's reemergence to *Star Trek*'s writer-producer Gene Roddenberry's follow-up, *Star Trek: The Next Generation* (1987–94). He writes, "The Golden Nineties of science fiction television could not have occurred without a groundbreaking predecessor like *TNG*, which did so much to reinvigorate the genre, proving that SFTV still had both ideas and audience appeal" (2012, 108–9). *Star Trek: TNG* was perceived as different, and thus better, than conventional science fiction, and, indeed, different from mainstream network shows. According to Howell, it was widely regarded as the first of a new generation of "quality" science fiction television (2017, 36). Its success led to *The X-Files* (1993–2002), whose authorial vision, merging of science fiction and horror, and visual style bears a strong relationship to *The Outer Limits*. The popularity of a show that combined science fiction and horror inspired the television remake of *The Outer Limits* (Showtime 1995–2001; SYFY 2002). But *The Outer Limits* remake, while providing a unique lens through which to view social and industrial changes between the 1960s and the 1990s, shows the limits placed upon science fiction in a commercial television landscape. In the contemporary era, the dystopian fiction *Black Mirror* (2011–), which grapples with the way digital technologies have transformed everyday experience (and not always for the better), takes on the mantel of the original *Outer Limits*. More so than any other recent program, *Black Mirror* brings *The Outer Limits'* warnings about technology, its fear of the power of media, and its ruminations on the human predicament into the modern era.

From *The Outer Limits* to *Star Trek*

Like Stevens and Stefano, Gene Roddenberry began writing for television during its "golden age" and was resistant to the limitations placed on writers and producers. He wrote for the dramatic anthologies *Four Star Playhouse* (1952–56) and *Kaiser Aluminum Hour* (1956–57), as well as critically acclaimed series such as *Have Gun Will Travel* (1957–63), *Naked City* (1960–63), and *Dr. Kildare* (1960–66). Like Stevens and Stefano, he was aware of the tensions between writers who wanted to produce socially relevant work and networks that wanted to make a profit. In his words, "The television writer-producer faces an almost impossible task when he [sic] attempts to create and produce a quality TV series. Assuming he conceived a program of such meaning and importance that it could ultimately change the face of America, he probably could not get it on the air or keep it there" (Whitfield and Roddenberry 1968, 1). But like Stevens and Stefano, Roddenberry saw science fiction as a way to convey serious ideas; as Whitfield explains, "By using science fiction yarns on far off planets, he was certain he could disguise the fact that he was actually talking about politics, sex, economics, the stupidity of war, and half a hundred other topics usually prohibited on television" (22). This was the modus operandi for *The Outer Limits*, and Roddenberry saw how it was done by visiting the set. Stefano's aide Tom Selden recalled, "*Star Trek* was in fact an outgrowth of *The Outer Limits*. Gene Roddenberry watched our dailies all the time and took a lot of phone calls from our screening room. He was spurring his imagination and checking on the incredible quality control we had. I wondered *why* he was there, but he was there more often than not during the time he was coming up with *Star Trek*" (Schow 1998, 324).

Similar to Stefano's "Canons," Roddenberry developed a detailed program outline for *Star Trek*. After several major studios turned the project down because it was too risky (i.e., potentially unprofitable), he successfully pitched it to Desilu. They sold the idea to NBC, and once the show was greenlit, Roddenberry hired several members of *The Outer Limits* production staff. Robert Justman, who had been an associate director on *The Outer Limits*, took over day-to-day producing duties. Justman recommended *Outer Limits* directors Byron Haskin and John Erman, as well as James Goldstone, who directed what became *Star Trek*'s pilot, "Where No Man Has Gone Before." Makeup artist Fred Phillips, monster designers Wah Chang and Janos Prohaska, and voice-over artist Robert Johnson provided continuity between monsters and props in the two series. Writers Meyer Dolinsky and Jerry Sohl worked on both series, and stars William Shatner and Leonard Nimoy had previously appeared on *The Outer Limits*. Shatner even played a space explorer in *The Outer Limit*'s season 2 episode "Cold Hands, Warm Heart" (though he was not the first choice for the lead role; he replaced actor Jeffrey Hunter, who left the series after NBC rejected the initial pilot, "The Cage").

Roddenberry described *Star Trek* as "*Wagon Train* to the stars," drawing on a popular television program that was structured as an ongoing westward journey with different adventures every week. Like *Wagon Train* (1957–62), *Star Trek* had continuing characters, though storylines remained in the anthology format. In Roddenberry's pitch to NBC, he claimed that *Star Trek* "is a new kind of television science fiction with all the advantages of an anthology, but none of the limitations" (Whitfield and Roddenberry 1968, 22–23). He also referred to the show as "*Gulliver's Travels* in space," reflecting his commitment, in the tradition of *The Outer Limits*, to both entertain and edify viewers through allegorical social commentary.

Justman's influence, similar creative personnel, and Roddenberry's objective to use science fiction for social commentary highlight the relationship between the two shows. In fact, *Star Trek*'s original pilot, "The Cage," may have been *too* similar to *The Outer Limits*: NBC considered it "too cerebral" and complained that the storyline was "too involved, too literate, and dwelt too much on intangibles" (Whitfield and Roddenberry 1968, 124). The second pilot, "Where No Man Has Gone Before," was more acceptable.

Star Trek is set in a future world where intergalactic nations, unified into a federation, live in social and political harmony. While *The Outer Limits* presents the alien "other" as more human than the humans, in the midst of the civil rights movement, *Star Trek* uses aliens to make allegorical arguments for racial equality and inclusivity. But in other ways, *Star Trek* is less critical than *The Outer Limits*. Perhaps more conducive to mainstream television, *Star Trek* is utopian and optimistic rather than bleak and dystopian. Instead of expressing anxieties about technology out of control or the dangers of overreaching science, *Star Trek* suggests that science and technology used ethically will benefit humankind. Franklin sums up its message:

> At the very least, as a relic of the height of the Cold War, *Star Trek* offers hope. Hope for a better future, hope for peace and hope for equality. All of these are realized in the unified crew of the Enterprise, with different people of different ethnicities and national origins working together. *Star Trek* presents a future where the people of the Earth overcome their differences and acknowledge

their common humanity, while celebrating their differences. (2008, 113)

Although their visions differ, both series make use of monsters and aliens and rely on visual and optical effects. *Star Trek*, shot in color, has little of the Gothic horror or noir science fiction elements that characterize *The Outer Limits* and does not aim to create terror. At the same time, many of the props and creatures from *The Outer Limits* were reused on *Star Trek*. In the first pilot episode, "The Cage," the creatures enclosed in the alien zoo had the same masks as those seen in *The Outer Limits* episodes "Fun and Games" and "Second Chance." To make Leonard Nimoy's pointed ears as Spock, makeup artist Fred Phillips replicated the process used to make alien ears in "The Sixth Finger." Even the transporter beam that became an iconic feature of *Star Trek* was first used in *The Outer Limits*' "The Mutant."

Other episodes repurposed props from *The Outer Limits*; recycling props and even footage was a common practice in science fiction programs. Roddenberry proposed keeping production costs under budget by "making creative use of whatever can be doubled over, stolen, and borrowed" (Whitfield and Roddenberry 1968, 296) Like *The Outer Limits*, *Star Trek* did not have a large budget, and props and monsters were expensive. Thus, Janos Prohaska, who both created and played a monster called the Horta in *The Outer Limits* episode "The Probe," modified the costume for *Star Trek*'s "Devil in the Dark." The pods that threatened to destroy humankind in "Specimen Unknown" reappeared in *Star Trek*'s "This Side of Paradise." The smoke ring effect from "Cold Hands, Warm Heart" was replicated in *Star Trek*'s "Balance of Terror," and the blob in "Counterweight" was similar to the one in *Star Trek*'s "Day of the Dove" (Harden 1980).

Props and monsters provided visual resemblances to *The Outer Limits*, but there were also thematic continuities, particularly in episodes written or directed by *Outer Limits* alumni. For example, *Star Trek's* season 3 episode "The Empath" was based on the 1933 science fiction novel *When Worlds Collide*. Its writer, Joyce Muskat, wanted it to be shot on a minimalist, surreal set that would allow a focus on the characters, which prompted Justman to hire John Erman, who had directed *The Outer Limits* episode "Nightmare" (discussed in chapter 2). Although the story lines are not identical, both episodes share the same theatrical quality, with a few characters interacting within an enclosed, sparsely decorated set. In both, an alien species observes and interrogates captives and submits them to torture in order to extract information. As in "Nightmare," there is a twist ending, where the aliens are revealed to be conducting an experiment. However, while "Nightmare" depicts fraying social bonds and documents the group's descent into barbarity, "The Empath" remains true to *Star Trek*'s utopian vision. Instead of turning upon each other, Captain Kirk, Dr. Spock, and Dr. McCoy attempt to sacrifice themselves in order to save the others. The ending of "Nightmare" presents the Earth's military as the real villains, but "The Empath" has no such political message. The twist in the latter case is that the aliens were conducting an experiment to determine whether the "empath" they had captured was compassionate enough to sacrifice herself for others. They tested her by torturing Dr. McCoy to see if she would take on his pain, and if she did, they would save her species. But rather than *The Outer Limits*' typical depiction of aliens as more evolved than the humans, Captain Kirk and Dr. Spock are the superior beings. They convince the aliens that because the empath has shown compassion, her species deserves to live. Rather than the grim ending of "Nightmare," "The Empath" resolves in a satisfying way.

Star Trek, like *The Outer Limits*, received mediocre ratings. NBC decided to cancel it at the end of season 2, but agreed to a third season after fans organized a letter-writing campaign. But, like Stefano, Roddenberry resigned as producer when NBC gave it an undesirable time slot on Fridays at 10 p.m., though he was still credited as executive producer. According to Schow, Roddenberry offered the job to Stefano, who turned it down (1998, 326). As Roddenberry predicted,

Star Trek was canceled at the end of season 3. But like *The Outer Limits*, it developed a cult following after it went into syndication. Through the years, it has reappeared in both films and television sequels, particularly the highly regarded *Star Trek: TNG* (1987–94), also produced by Roddenberry. One of its most controversial episodes was "Skin of Evil," reviled by many fans because a main character was ignominiously killed off. The story was conceived and written by Joseph Stefano.

The Outer Limits and "Quality" Science Fiction

Howell argues that one of the ways science fiction became legitimated as "quality" television in the late 1980s was by distancing itself from its low-culture generic origins. *The Outer Limits* first illustrated how this could be done by combining lowbrow science fiction with expressionist and surrealistic forms of artistic expression, incorporating literary themes and plots, and evoking its links to the dramatic anthology series of the 1950s. Stefano and Stevens were independent producer-writers who used the formal characteristics of the medium to convey a vision. Similarly, years later *The X-Files'* blend of science fiction and horror, its formal characteristics, its thematic concerns, and its association with a single creative source marked it as both quality television and a successor to *The Outer Limits*.

Both *The X-Files* and *The Outer Limits* merge science fiction and horror. According to Johnson, *The X-Files'* hybridity established it as distinctive. "Furthermore," she adds, "the series' sophisticated scripts, complex multilayered narratives, and visually expressive cinematography, combined with its exploration of contemporary anxieties concerning late capitalism (such as *The X-Files'* treatment of environmental issues, the role of medicine, the threat of scientific experimentation, and most overtly, the duplicity of the US government) is characteristic of quality television" (2005, 99–100). *The X-Files'* creator, writer, and producer, Chris Carter, claimed that the show was meant to redress the lack of horror on television and to scare viewers (quoted in Johnson 2005, 101), much as *The Outer Limits* aimed to frighten and unsettle viewers years before. In order to do so, *The X-Files'* visual style, like that of *The Outer Limits*, makes use of low-key lighting, shadows, strong contrasts, and moody atmospherics characteristic of film noir and Gothic horror, an expressive style that had virtually disappeared from television after its transition to color.

Structurally, *The X-Files* combines an ongoing narrative arc with stand-alone "monster of the week" episodes. Like *The Outer Limits*, the monster episodes rely on special effects and horrific creatures. While in *The Outer Limits* the humans are depicted as more "monstrous" than the monsters, *The X-Files* slightly shifts the emphasis of the critique. Geller suggests that in *The X-Files*, "The MOTW episodes introduce a wide array of Others to examine the way these Others are construed as 'monstrous' by normal society" (2016, 15). Geller also observes that like all science fiction, *The X-Files* grounded its concerns in the present day and engaged with sociopolitical realities (62). She compares its social commentary to that of earlier TV horror programs (though she omits *The Outer Limits*): "What these shows share with *The X-Files* are more than horror's thrilling transgressions: they were openly concerned with the social landscape in America, and were able to generate social commentary under the guise of horror, because, although horror is a consistently popular genre, it is also among the more disreputable, seen as pure 'entertainment'" (41). Chris Carter, who was creator, producer, and sometimes writer, describes his vision in terms that evoke *The Outer Limits*: "We are living in a world where technological and medical advancements are making quantum leaps. We don't quite know how to fathom these things and it gives us a feeling we may not be in control" (Garcia and Phillips 2008). *The X-Files* replicates *The Outer Limits'* warnings about technology and pessimism regarding scientific "progress," its critique of the military-industrial complex (expressed through a narrative about government corruption and conspiracies), and its questioning of the "nature" of human nature, particularly in MOTW episodes. In both shows, science fiction and horror—traditionally considered low-culture forms—merge form and content to become socially relevant "quality" television.

The New *Outer Limits*

At the same time that *The Outer Limits* paved the way for *The X-Files*, the success of *The X-Files* sparked the reboot of *The Outer Limits* that aired on Showtime (and, in its final season, SYFY) from 1995 to 2002 (Geller 2016, 14). After a failed initial attempt to revive *The Outer Limits* in the 1980s, in 1995 MGM (who owned the rights along with Stevens and Stefano) partnered with a Canadian American film company, Trilogy Entertainment, to create a new series. Although the new version lasted for seven seasons, it was less an exemplar of innovative television than an illustration of industry constraints in an increasingly competitive television landscape.

Executive producer Richard B. Lewis acknowledged that the new *Outer Limits* had more to do with branding than a shared sensibility with the older show (Schow 1998, 345). The producers brought Stevens and Stefano onto the series in advisory roles to lend it their imprimatur (and also because they needed both men's permission in order to use the title). But, as Stefano noted, their positions were largely honorary (Counts 1997, 70). The differences between the two versions are signified by the opening Control Voice, who speaks two new additional two lines: "We can deluge you with a thousand channels or expand one single image to crystal clarity and beyond. We can shape your vision to anything our imagination can conceive." *LA Times* reporter Arion Berger writes, "This narration seems to come not from aliens or demons, beings whose thought processes differ from ours, but from rich, greedy old men. It's the programmer's credo: mind control, dissemination of handsome garbage, product placement, Q ratings, twist endings" (quoted in Schow 1998, 346). Rather than instilling fear of television as an "alien" presence, the new lines serve as a reminder that television is a commercial medium dependent on viewers.

Because the new series aired on a premium cable network, producers could—and did—include female nudity, though with an eye to how it could be cut if the show was syndicated. They also ratcheted up the violence. In the original *Outer Limits* there were frequent deaths, but not gory ones; scenes of torture were never explicit or drawn out as they were in the new version. Rather, the horror was off-screen, made all the more frightening by what was implied but not seen (a technique also characteristic of *The X-Files*). The new show also relied less on monsters and aliens than the original, though it made extensive use of CGI and other special effects technologies at the forefront of televised science fiction. It was still structured as an anthology, although several episodes had overlapping storylines, and most season finales contained clips that recycled material from previous episodes, a technique emulated in *Black Mirror*'s 2017 fourth-season finale, "Black Museum."

The philosophical probing and bleak vision that characterized the original *Outer Limits* was replaced by a more moralistic tone. According to producer Sam Egan, referring to the new series, "The core of every *Outer Limits* episode is a parable, a morality tale" (Counts 1997, 70). The new show even had a different "Bible," a fifteen-page document defining the show as "tales of science gone wrong" and written without reference to Stefano's "Canons." Stories focused on scientists experimenting with new technologies, time travel, encounters with hostile aliens, or flights to other worlds, while maintaining the original's stylistic emphasis on science fiction "Gothic horror" (Garcia and Phillips 2008).

Differences between the two series are apparent in the one episode where Stefano took an active role by remaking "A Feasibility Study," which he had originally written and produced in 1964. Producer Egan spoke to the idea of a remake: "It's this notion of a bridge to the past. The kind of storytelling that made the original series a success is really the same kind of storytelling that we're involved with in this se-
110 ries" (Garcia and Phillips 2008). In the 1997 version, slightly renamed

"Feasibility Study," Stefano appears to have some latitude with updating the story. Both versions share the same premise: an alien species searching for slave labor transports a suburban neighborhood to their planet to see if people from earth can survive in their atmosphere. In 1964, Stefano used a science fiction context to portray the disillusionment of postwar suburbia, characterized by disintegrating marriages and social isolation, along with a critique of capitalism and materialist values. In the earlier version, the aliens need workers to perform physical labor because they have been calcified by a virus that immobilizes them. In a metaphor for the isolation that characterized postwar suburban communities, as long as people do not touch the aliens, or one another, they will remain free of contagion. The aliens attempt to lure the earthlings with promises of comfort and prosperity in exchange for enslavement, mirroring the false promises of consumer culture that depend on the acquiescence of the middle class.

But the episode is most famous for its climax. The members of the neighborhood, made aware that the aliens intend to enslave the earth's population, gather in a church. The main character, Simon, criticizes their isolated existence and argues for the importance of communal bonds and a sense of collective purpose. Rather than submit to enslavement, they can save the rest of the planet if they act in solidarity for the greater good by infecting themselves with the virus. Simon joins hands with his formerly estranged wife, who is already infected. One by one, the group joins hands in a gesture of self-sacrifice. The episode ends with a freeze frame, with the community now calcified in stone. ABC censor Dorothy Brown initially refused to allow the episode to air because she thought it condoned mass suicide, though she relented eight months after it was initially scheduled. The ending, while an affirmation of human community, was typically bleak and disturbing.

The 1997 episode stars David McCallum, to whom Stefano reached out because he had been in two of the original *Outer Limits* episodes, "The Sixth Finger" and "The Forms of Things Unknown." Stefano said that he was drawn to the new version of the story because its central theme still had relevance: "For me, it was the show's eternal theme of people sacrificing themselves for the good of others. . . . I thought it was something we ought to be hearing, especially now, since we don't seem to have a strong sense of heroes anymore" (Counts 1997, 70). The new episode deepens the representation of alienation and the disintegration of familial and social bonds begun in 1964. In 1997, the suburban neighborhood is replaced by a gated community. The enclosed world designed to exclude those who do not belong is policed by a black security guard; virtually the only person of color in the community, he is a reminder of earth's own systems of oppression. Moreover, the nuclear family has almost entirely disappeared. In the earlier version the main conflict involved Simon and his wife separating because she saw marriage as a "prison." Here the main character is Joshua, whose wife has already left him to raise their teenage daughter, Sarah, alone. A rift in the father-daughter relationship further serves as a metaphor for the dysfunctional family.

Members of the community are not just isolated from one another, but the fragile social order threatens to erupt into chaos. When faced with fear and uncertainty, a mob forms, and they accuse one neighbor of hoarding food and power—a scene that recalls *The Twilight Zone*'s "The Monsters are Due on Maple Street" (1960), another example of fear leading to social disintegration. Joshua drives the point home in the midst of a quarrel with Sarah: "Entropy. That's what they call it when everything starts breaking down."

"Feasibility Study" also illustrates the development of special effects from the 1960s to the 1990s. Instead of the low-tech fog that enshrouded the neighborhood in 1964, it is now surrounded by a shimmering force field, and when the neighborhood is transported, a spectacular CGI special effect shows it hurtling through the sky. The barren landscape looks naturalistic rather than theatrically artificial, and the alien prosthetics—while owing a debt to the earlier work of Project Unlimited—are far more sophisticated. The climax is also much more visual than in the original. The community gathers to hear from those who have had contact with the aliens; unlike his predecessor, Simon, when Joshua speaks he does not emphasize communal bonds or collective purpose so much as advocate their freedom and choice not to become enslaved—a telling change in the individualist context of 1990s neoliberalism. But again, everyone in the community slowly joins hands and dooms themselves to save the rest of the human race. The final image encourages the viewer to linger: a slow-motion montage is punctuated by dramatic, emotional music, followed by a final sequence of still images of the group, now petrified in stone. The Control Voice drives the message home: "For centuries, philosophers and theologians have debated what it means to be human. Perhaps it has eluded us because it is so simple. To be human is to choose." His explanation shifts their motivation from the altruistic concern for the community to the expression of individual agency. The philosophical probing that characterized the original *Outer Limits* is replaced by a definition of human nature that reflects rather than criticizes the politics of the era.

Overall, "Feasibility Study" portrays a society where personal relationships are largely dysfunctional or nonexistent, and where the social order has broken down amid an exploitative universe. But in accord with the moralistic tone of the new series, the final scene serves as an admonition that leaves no ambiguity. Unlike the original series, the conclusion discourages rather than encourages critical thought. As producer Richard B. Lewis explained in a Showtime interview:

I think that one of the reasons *Outer Limits* works for us is we're dealing with essential moral issues . . . our goal is to raise those issues and inject our own sense of morality. If you do things wrong from what your parents tell you, you're going to be scared to death; terrible things are going to happen to you. So we make films about that, setting the mores of the times. And if you do take that step into areas you know are wrong, there's going to be punishment, and I think that is the way society works. (We) reinforce the sense of community, and the right set of rules to live by. (Schow 1998, 347)

It is unclear how much control Stefano had over the final version of the episode. But he seemed critical of the process. Afterward he wrote,

The writer's freedoms today are not any different than in the 1960s as far as content. The same rules and laws apply today as they did then. There are still things they don't like and won't have in the script. There's a great myth about the freedom of cable television. It's bullshit, frankly. It's not there. It depends on who is running what. The people who are running these have their own attitudes, their own tastes, about what should be on television. So we're no different today than we were in the 1960s. As a matter of fact, there are more people today censoring and telling us what we should do. (Garcia and Phillips 2008)

Television and culture had changed since the 1960s, and clearly the producers saw their mission as providing moral guidance rather than—in the best tradition of *The Outer Limits*—inducing "awe or wonder or tolerable terror or even merely conversation and argument" (Schow 1998, 354).

Into the Future: *The Outer Limits* and *Black Mirror*

The Outer Limits' central themes and concerns, rooted in the anxiety induced by the social and political transformations of the post–World War II era, are even more relevant in the twenty-first century. In the context of the early 1960s, *The Outer Limits* inspires critical thinking about the meaning of technology, whether in the electronic medium of television, the rise of the military-industrial complex, or the possibility of nuclear annihilation. It addresses fears and anxieties in the midst of social and cultural transformation and ponders broader philosophical questions about human nature. In the contemporary television landscape, there may be less need to couch social and political commentary in allegorical terms, but perhaps more need for cultural forms to come to grips with the role that technology plays in our lives. In this regard, the dystopian anthology series *Black Mirror*, which considers the way digital technologies have transformed everyday experience, can best be compared to *The Outer Limits*. Vander-Meer's description of *Black Mirror* could equally be applied to *The Outer Limits*: an "anthology series based on what you might call 'an acute examination of dysfunctional tech horrors or the horror-implications of said tech'" (2016).

While *Black Mirror* is frequently related to *The Twilight Zone*, its grounding in science fiction merged with horror, its reliance on special effects, and its focus on humans' complicated relationship with technology has far more in common with *The Outer Limits*. The connection between the two is apparent in their respective opening credits. Like those of *The Outer Limits*, *Black Mirror*'s credits self-reflexively draw attention to technology—in the case of *The Outer Limits*, it is the television, while in *Black Mirror*, it is the digital screen. According to creator Charlie Brooker, "It's the screen of the devices that we use every day—TV, computers, tablets, and smartphones, when they are

Images from *Black Mirror* opening credits.

turned off" (Affatigato 2019). Both sets of credits are meant to disturb viewers. *Black Mirror*'s simple black-and-white opening—a callback to earlier anthology series—is a black screen, followed by images of disruption: a distorted sound effect, a spinning "throbber" that indicates buffering, and the inscrutable letters of a scrambled signal. The letters cohere into the title "Black Mirror," followed by a crack like that of a phone screen. The fractured images are similar to the interference patterns of the credits of *The Outer Limits*.

But the television screen from the 1960s has been replaced by a mirror. Instead of merely stoking fear that technology has the potential to control us, *Black Mirror* suggests that our technologies reflect our beliefs and behaviors back to us. Rather than technology existing apart from the humans who use it, the implication is that we are responsible for its use and misuse. Keslowitz summarizes its message: "*Black Mirror* explores the moral implications of developing technology, forces us to confront truths about where humanity is now, and looking forward, how it could be tipped into murkier waters" (2020, 3).

Whereas *The Outer Limits* expresses fears about technology that has exceeded our ability to control it, and its stories often feature scientists or inventors who find themselves in situations that spiral out of control, *Black Mirror* expresses anxieties about digital culture and similarly deals with "ordinary individuals who have been granted extraordinary powers by new technologies, but have yet to recognize their responsibilities and the technology's unexpected ramifications" (Saler 2019). For example, "USS Callister" (2017), one of the most famous episodes of *Black Mirror*, is a parody of *Star Trek* that also relies on many of the science fiction tropes seen in *The Outer Limits*. It takes the figure of the outsider obsessed with technological "tinkering" seen in episodes such as "The Galaxy Being" and turns him into a gamer, Robert Daly, a loner who invents a virtual reality game that he populates with copies of his colleagues. He tortures them, demands affection from the women, and turns some of them into spider monsters. The monsters, called Arachnajax, resemble the creatures in *The Outer Limits* episode "Zanti Misfits" (1963). And, of course, the true monster is the villainous Daly.

Many episodes of *Black Mirror* distance themselves from science fiction in favor of a more realistic, if dystopian, depiction of everyday life. For example, Brooker has famously stated that episodes are "all about the way we live now—and the way we might be living in ten minutes' time if we're clumsy" (2011). But "USS Callister" is an unusual episode because it embraces classic science fiction: it relies on special effects, futuristic devices, monsters, spaceships, otherworldly settings, and more contemporary tropes such as cloning and AI. It pays homage to *Star Trek*, particularly in its reproduction of 1960s-style costumes and even the spaceship, but otherwise its iconography, themes, and concerns are built on those introduced in *The Outer Limits*. In particular, the fear of television's "electronic nowhere" (Sconce 1997, 23) is manifest here by depicting cyberspace as a literal space where people are entrapped. While in some ways "USS Callister" ends happily, with a female-led crew who control their own destinies in a new virtual reality game, the concerns it raises about VR and cyberspace and the way we use technology remain unresolved. Like *The Outer Limits*, *Black Mirror* allows viewers to grapple with real fears in the guise of entertainment.

Conclusion

The Outer Limits led the way for televised science fiction that was smart, innovative, and provocative. It came on the air during a moment of industrial transition, when its creators, Joseph Stefano and Leslie Stevens, had to circumvent network executives in order to make meaningful statements and to create art that both entertained and edified viewers. Turning to genre fiction allowed Stevens and Stefano to make social and political commentary in a commercial context that eschewed challenging or controversial material. In terms of formal properties, its admixture of noir science fiction and Gothic horror merged theatrical and cinematic expressionism. In so doing, it demonstrated televisuality long before other television programs embraced an expressive visual style. In the guise of science fiction-based horror, *The Outer Limits* provided a way for viewers to contemplate an increasingly complex cultural landscape. It served as a counterpoint to the reassuring narratives that typified television programs in the 1960s, as it addressed the anxieties that marked the postwar period and challenged the New Frontier's optimism and faith in technology. Its pessimistic view of fear and aggression at the heart of human nature and bleak endings that warned of the dire consequences of technology run amok paved the way for the dystopian fiction of later shows. Through creative adaptation, familiar forms and genres were transformed into art that commented on the present and expressed *The Outer Limits'* unique vision. But, as we have seen, Stefano's final adaptation, "The Forms of Things Unknown," demonstrated the constraints imposed upon the writer-producer whose ideas conflict with network imperatives.

Overall, *The Outer Limits* demonstrated the power of compelling stories to articulate inchoate hopes and fears and to simultaneously entertain and provoke thought. All of its brethren from *Star Trek* to *Black Mirror* continue to address the relationship between humans and technology; all continue to ask what it means to be human in an increasingly complex world. *The Outer Limits* pondered the question by looking at, rather than away from, cultural anxieties and tensions, and although what it revealed was not always reassuring, it paved the way for such stories to be told.

REFERENCES

Affatigato, Carlo. 2019. "The True Meaning of Black Mirror." Auralcrave, February 7, 2019. https://auralcrave.com/en/2019/02/07/the-true-meaning-of-black-mirror/.

Alexander, David. 1991. Interview with Gene Roddenberry. The Humanist, March–April 1991. https://thehumanist.com/features/interviews/humanist-interview-gene-roddenberry (accessed May 14, 2021).

Alvey, Mark. 1997. "The Independents: Rethinking the Television Studio System." In *The Revolution Wasn't Televised*, edited by Lynn Spigel and Michael Curtin, 139–60. New York: Routledge.

Anderson, Chris. 1994. *Hollywood TV: The Studio System in the Fifties*. Austin: University of Texas Press.

Barnouw, Eric. 1962. *The Television Writer*. New York: Hill & Wang.

——. 1975. *Tube of Plenty: The Evolution of American Television*. New York: Oxford University Press.

Baughman, James L. 2007. *Same Time, Same Station: Creating American Television, 1948–1961*. Baltimore, MD: Johns Hopkins University Press.

Baxter, John. 1970. *Science Fiction in the Cinema*. New York: Paperback Library.

Beam, Craig. 2014. "Episode Spotlight: 'Forms of Things Unknown.'" My Life in the Glow of *The Outer Limits*. http://mylifeintheglowoftheouterlimits.blogspot.com/2014/05/episode-spotlight-forms-of-things.html (accessed May 14, 2021).

———. 2013. "Episode Spotlight: 'The Architects of Fear.'" My Life in the Glow of *The Outer Limits*. http://mylifeintheglowoftheouterlimits.blogspot.com/2013/09/episode-spotlight-architects-of-fear.html (accessed July 8, 2021).

Berger, Maurice. 2014. *Revolution of the Eye: Modern Art and the Birth of American Television*. New Haven, CT: Yale University Press.

Blamire, Larry. 2011. "Spotlight on 'Nightmare.'" We Are Controlling Transmission. http://wearecontrollingtransmission.blogspot.com (accessed July 8, 2021).

Boddy, William. 1993. *Fifties Television: The Industry and its Critics*. Urbana: University of Illinois Press.

Booker, M. Keith. 2001. *Monsters, Mushroom Clouds, and the Cold War: American Science Fiction and the Roots of Postmodernism, 1946–1964*. Westport, CT: Greenwood.

———. 2004. *Science Fiction Television*. Westport, CT: Praeger.

———. 2012. "*Star Trek* and the Birth of a Film Franchise." In *Science Fiction Film, Television, and Adaptation*, edited by J. P. Telotte and Gerald Duchovny, 101–14. New York: Routledge.

Bould, Mark. 2003. "Film and Television." In *The Cambridge Companion to Science Fiction*, edited by Edward James and Farah Mendleson, 79–95. Cambridge: Cambridge University Press.

Brennan, David. n.d. "The Ellison Dispute." http://www.jamescamerononline.com/Ellison.htm (accessed May 14, 2021).

Brooker, Charlie. 2011. "Charlie Brooker: The Dark Side of Our Gadget Addiction." *Guardian*, December 1, 2011. https://www.theguardian.com/technology/2011/dec/01/charlie-brooker-dark-side-gadget-addiction-black-mirror.

Caldwell, John Thornton. 1995. *Televisuality: Style, Crisis, and Authority in American Television*. New Brunswick, NJ: Rutgers University Press.

Canavan, Gerry, and Eric Carl Link. 2015. "Introduction." In *The Cambridge Companion to American Science Fiction*, 1–13. Cambridge: Cambridge University Press.

Cherry, Brigid. 2014. "Gothic on the Small Screen." In *The Gothic World*, edited by Glennis Byron and Dale Townshend, 487–97. New York: Routledge.

Cochran, David. 2010. *America Noir: American Writers and Filmmakers of the Postwar Era*. Washington, DC: Smithsonian.

Counts, Kyle. 1997. "A New Feasibility Study." *Starlog*, August 1997, 70–73.

Deighan, Samm. 2016. "Moral Degenerates: Rediscovering Leslie Steven's Private Property." *Diabolique Magazine*, July 5, 2016. https://diaboliquemagazine

.com/moral-degenerates-rediscovering-leslie-stevens-private-property -1960/.

Everett, Anna. 2013. "'Golden Age' of Television Drama." In *Encyclopedia of Television*, vol. 2, 2nd ed., edited by Horace Newcomb, 1001–4. New York: Routledge.

Faust, Christa. 2011. "Spotlight on 'The Bellero Shield.'" We Are Controlling Transmission, February 11, 2011. http://wearecontrollingtransmission.blogspot .com/2011/02/spotlight-on-bellero-shield.html.

Franklin, Morris Emory III. 2008. "Do Not Attempt to Adjust the Picture: The Cold War Crisis of Liberal Democracy and Science Fiction Television." PhD diss., University of Utah.

French, Sean. 1996. *The Terminator*. London: BFI.

Garcia, Mark, and Frank Phillips. 2008. *Science Fiction Television Series, 1990–2004*. Jefferson, NC: McFarland.

Geller, Teresa L. 2016. *The X-Files*. Detroit, MI: Wayne State University Press.

Gerani, Gary. 1977. "The Inner Mind of *The Outer Limits*." *Starlog*, March 1977, 54–56.

——. 2011. "Spotlight on 'Forms of Things Unknown.'" We Are Controlling Transmission, February 15, 2011. http://wearecontrollingtransmission.blogspot .com/2011/02/spotlight-on-forms-of-things-unknown.html.

Glover, Allen. 2019. *TV Noir: Dark Drama on the Small Screen*. New York: Abrams.

Gomery, Douglas. 1992. *Shared Pleasures: A History of Movie Presentation in the United States*. Madison: University of Wisconsin Press.

Grant, Barry Keith. 2020. *The Twilight Zone*. Detroit, MI: Wayne State University Press.

Harden, Dan. 1980. "The Outer Limits Connection: *Star Trek* Myths, Pt. 2." *Stardate* 7, December 1980. http://www.orionpressfanzines.com/articles/ startrekmyths2.htm (accessed May 14, 2021).

Hill, Rodney. 2008. "Anthology Drama." In *The Essential Science Fiction Television Reader*, edited by J. P. Telotte, 111–26. Lexington: University Press of Kentucky.

Hilmes, Michele. 1990. *Hollywood and Broadcasting: From Radio to Cable*. Champaign: University of Illinois Press.

Holcomb, Mark. 2002. "The Outer Limits." Salon, April 9, 2002. https://www .salon.com/2002/04/09/outer_limits/.

Holcomb, Mark, and David Holcomb. 2008a. The Fashion of Dreaming: A Critical Guide to *The Outer Limits*. https://web.archive.org/web/20190103034520/ http://home.earthlink.net/%7Emarkholcomb/ol/front.html#close (accessed May 14, 2021).

———. 2008b. "Nightmare." The Fashion of Dreaming. https://web.archive.org/web/20180606042849/http://home.earthlink.net/~markholcomb/ol/ol_nightmare.html (accessed May 14, 2021).

Horrocks, Chris. 2017. *The Joy of Sets: A Short History of the Television*. London: Reaktion.

Howell, Charlotte E. 2017. "Legitimating Genre: The Discursive Turn to Quality in Early 1990s Science Fiction Television." *Critical Studies in Television* 12, no. 1: 35–50.

Hutchings, Peter. 2018. "Pigeons from Hell: Anthology Horror on American Television in the 1950s and 1960s." In *Horror Television in the Age of Consumption: Binging on Fear*, edited by Linda Belau and Kimberly Jackson, 16–28. New York: Routledge.

Jancovich, Mark. 2108. "Where It Belongs: Television Horror, Domesticity, and *Alfred Hitchcock Presents*." In *Horror Television in the Age of Consumption: Binging on Fear*, edited by Linda Belau and Kimberly Jackson, 29–44. New York: Routledge.

Johnson, Catherine. 2005. *Telefantasy*. London: BFI.

Johnson Smith, Jan. 2005. *American Science Fiction*. Middletown, CT: Wesleyan University Press.

Jowett, Lorna, and Stacy Abbott. 2013. *TV Horror: Investigating the Dark Side of the Small Screen*. London: I. B. Tauris.

Keslowitz, Steven. 2020. *The Digital Dystopias of Black Mirror and Electric Dreams*. Jefferson, NC: McFarland.

King, Susan. 2000. "An Original Writer Talks of Creating 'Limits.'" *LA Times*, March 9, 2000, https://www.latimes.com/archives/la-xpm-2000-mar-09-ca-6841-story.html.

Kraszewski, Jon. 2010. *The New Entrepreneurs: An Institutional History of Television Anthology Writers*. Middletown, CT: Wesleyan University Press.

Ledwon, Leonora. 1993. "*Twin Peaks* and the Television Gothic." *Literature/Film Quarterly* 21, no. 4: 260–70.

Link, Eric Carl, and Gerry Canavan. 2015. "Introduction." In *The Cambridge Companion to American Science Fiction*, edited by Eric Carl Link and Gerry Canavan, 1–16. New York: Cambridge University Press.

Lucas, Tim. 2018. Commentary, "Forms of Things Unknown." *The Outer Limits*. Blu-ray. New York: Kino Lorber.

May, Elaine Tyler. 1999. *Homeward Bound: American Families in the Cold War Era*. New York: Basic Books.

Meehan, Paul. 2008. *Tech-Noir: The Fusion of Science Fiction and Film Noir*. Jefferson, NC: McFarland.

Meeler, Paul, and Eric Hill. 2015. "Sharing Social Context: Is Community with the Postmodern Possible?" In *The Palgrave Handbook of Film and Television*, edited by Michael Hauskeller, Thomas D. Philbeck, and Curtis D. Carbonell, 279–88. London: Palgrave Macmillan.

Miller, Cynthia. 2012. "Domesticating Space: Science Fiction Serials Come Home." In *Science Fiction, Film, and Adaptation*, edited by J. P. Telotte and Gerald Duchovny, 3–19. New York: Routledge.

Muir, John Kenneth. "*The Outer Limits*: 'The Guests.'" John Kenneth Muir's Reflections on Cult Movies and Classic TV, January 9, 2014. http://reflectionsonfilmandtelevision.blogspot.com/2014/01/the-outer-limits-guests.html.

Murray, Doug. 1987. The Outer Limits *Files: Specimen Unknown*. Canoga Park, CA: Psi Fi Movie.

Newcomb, Horace. 1997. "The Opening of America: Meaningful Difference in 1950s Television." In *The Other Fifties: Interrogating Midcentury American Icons*, edited by Joel Foreman, 103–23. Champaign: University of Illinois Press.

"New Wavelet." 1960. *Time*, May 23, 1960, 69.

Prawer, S. S. 1980. *Caligari's Children: The Film as Tale of Terror*. Oxford: Oxford University Press.

Rapchack, Larry. 2011. "Spotlight on 'Architects of Fear.'" We Are Controlling Transmission, January 7, 2011. http://wearecontrollingtransmission.blogspot.com/2011/01/spotlight-on-architects-of-fear.html.

Rypel, Ted. 1977. *The Outer Limits: An Illustrated Review*. Vol. 1. Cleveland, OH: Scorpio 13.

Saler, Michael. 2019. "A 'Mirror' to Our Souls." *Weekly Standard*, April 20, 2019. https://www.washingtonexaminer.com/weekly-standard/a-mirror-to-our-souls.

Samerdyke, Michael. 2017. *Horror 213*. Vol. 2. Self-published.

Sarris, Andrew. 1985. *The American Cinema: Directors and Directions, 1929–1968*. Chicago: Dutton.

Schow, David. 1998. *The Outer Limits Companion*. 2nd ed. Hollywood, CA: GNP/Crescendo.

References

———. 2018. DVD booklet. *The Outer Limits*. Season 2. New York: Kino Lorber.

Schrader, Paul. 1972. "Notes on Film Noir." *Film Comment* 8, no. 1: 581–92.

Sconce, Jeffrey. 1997. "The 'Outer Limits' of Oblivion." In *The Revolution Wasn't Televised: Sixties Television and Social Conflict*, edited by Lynn Spigel and Michael Curtin, 21–45. Minneapolis: University of Minnesota Press.

Shannon, Jeff. 2011. "A Master Emerges: Conrad Hall and *The Outer Limits*." Roger Ebert, September 27, 2011. https://www.rogerebert.com/demanders/a -master-emerges-conrad-hall-and-the-outer-limits.

Sontag, Susan. 1965. "The Imagination of Disaster." *Commentary*, October 1965, 42–48.

Spigel, Lynn. 1991. "From Domestic Space to Outer Space: The 1960s Television Fantastic Family Sitcom." In *Close Encounters: Film, Feminism, and Science Fiction*, edited by Constance Penley, Elisabeth Lyon, Lynn Spigel, and Janet Bergstrom, 205–36. Minneapolis: University of Minnesota Press.

Stefano, Joseph. 1963. *The Outer Limits*: "The Bellero Shield" teleplay. https:// dailyscript.com/scripts/outer_limits_bellero_shield1.pdf (accessed July 9, 2021).

Stefano, Joseph, Robert Justman, Lou Morheim, and David Schow. *"The Outer Limits."* Talk at Paley Center Television Festival, March 10, 2000, Los Angeles, California.

Telotte, J. P. 2012. "Introduction: Across the Screens: Adaptation, Boundaries, and Science Fiction Film and Television." In *Science Fiction Film, Television, and Adaptation: Across the Screens*, edited by J. P. Telotte and Gerald Duchovny, xiii–ix. New York: Routledge.

Telotte, J. P., ed. 2008. *The Essential Science Fiction Television Reader*. Lexington: University of Kentucky Press.

Troyan, Douglas. 1993. "'You are about to participate in a great adventure': Science, Scientists, and the Spectator in *The Outer Limits*." In *Spectator*, edited by Steven Tropiano and Marsha Kinder, 62–71. Los Angeles: University of Southern California Press.

Tudor, Andrew. 1989. *Monsters and Mad Scientists: A Cultural History of the Horror Film*. Cambridge: Basil Blackwell.

Ursini, James. 1999. "Noir Science." In *Film Noir Reader 2*, edited by Alain Silver and James Ursini, 223–42. New York: Limelight.

VanderMeer, Jeff. 2016. "The Complex Humanity of Black Mirror." *Atlantic*, October 29, 2016. https://www.theatlantic.com/entertainment/archive/ 2016/10/the-complex-humanity-of-black-mirror/505811/.

Variety. 1960. "Is There an American 'New Wave'?" March 30, 1960, 4.

Vianello, Robert. 2013. "The Rise of the Telefilm and the Network's Hegemony over the Motion Picture Industry." In *New Directions in Television History and Theory*, edited by Nick Browne, 3–22. New York: Routledge.

Wasson, Sara, and Emily Alder. 2011. *Gothic Science Fiction, 1980–2010.* Liverpool: Liverpool University Press.

Westfahl, Gary. 1999. *The Mechanics of Wonder: The Creation of the Idea of Science Fiction.* Liverpool: Liverpool University Press.

Wheatley, Helen. A. 2006. *Gothic Television.* Manchester: Manchester University Press.

Whitfield, Stephen E., and Gene Roddenberry. 1968. *The Making of* Star Trek. New York: Ballantine.

Wildermuth, Mark. 2014. *Gender, Science Fiction Television, and the American Security State: 1958–Present.* New York: Palgrave MacMillan.

Willaert, Kate. 2015. "Did *Watchmen* Steal from *The Outer Limits*, or from Jack Kirby?" The Beat: The Blog of Comics Culture, August 10, 2015. https://www.comicsbeat.com/did-watchmen-steal-from-the-outer-limits-or-from-jack-kirby/.

Wissner, Reba A. 2016. *We Will Control All That Your Hear: The Outer Limits and the Aural Imagination.* Hillsdale, NY: Pendragon.

Worland, Eric John. 1989. *The Other Living Room War: Evolving Cold War Imagery in Popular Programs of the Vietnam Era, 1960–1975.* PhD diss., University of California, Los Angeles.

"Writing *Psycho*: Interview with Joseph Stefano." 2019. Diary of a Screenwriter, March 11, 2019. http://diaryofascreenwriter.blogspot.com/2018/09/writing-psycho-interview-with-joseph.html.

Yaszek, Lisa. 2008. "Shadows on the Cathode Ray Tube: Adapting Print Science Fiction for Television." In *The Essential Science Fiction Television Reader*, edited by J. P. Telotte, 55–67. Lexington: University of Kentucky Press.

INDEX

9 780814 347454